THE NEW HACKER'S HANDBOOK

THE NEW HACKER'S HANDBOOK

HUGO CORNWALL

CENTURY
LONDON MELBOURNE AUCKLAND JOHANNESBURG

Copyright © Hugo Cornwall 1985, 1986

All rights reserved

First published in 1985 as
The Hacker's Handbook, revised edition 1986,
by Century Hutchinson Ltd.,
Brookmount House, 62-65 Chandos Place,
Covent Garden, London WC2N 4NW

Century Hutchinson Publishing Group (Australia) Pty Ltd
16-22 Church Street, Hawthorn, Melbourne, Victoria 3122

Century Hutchinson Group (NZ) Ltd
32-34 View Road, PO Box 40-086, Glenfield, Auckland 10

Century Hutchinson Group (SA) Pty Ltd
PO Box 337, Bergvlei 2012, South Africa

ISBN 0 7126 9711 X

Photoset in North Wales by
Derek Doyle & Associates, Mold, Clwyd
Printed and bound in Great Britain by
Richard Clay (The Chaucer Press) Ltd, Bungay, Suffolk

CONTENTS

	Introduction	vii
1	First Principles	1
2	Computer-to-Computer Communications	8
3	Hackers' Equipment	19
4	Targets	35
5	Hackers' Intelligence	49
6	Hackers' Techniques	66
7	Networks	80
8	Videotex Systems	97
9	Radio Computer Data	109
10	Hacking: The Future	122

Appendices

I	Trouble Shooting	130
II	Eclectic Glossary	135
III	Selected CCITT Recommendations	145
IV	Computer Alphabets	147
V	Modems and Services	156
VI	RS232C and V.24	161
VII	The Radio Spectrum	164
VIII	Port-Finder Flow Chart	168

INTRODUCTION

During 1985 the original *Hacker's Handbook* went through a remarkable number of reprints. It seemed to both publisher and author that, rather than pushing the old plates through the printing press yet one more time, we should sit back and reflect whether extensive revisions were not called for.

1985 will, I believe, be identified by future historians of such matters as rather crucial in the history of the development of personal computing power. 1984 was the last year in which it was at all reasonable for a manufacturer to offer for sale a home computer lacking the essential facility of being able to pick up information from, and talk to, the outside world. From 1986 onward only pure games computers, or those designed for very specific purposes, will lack proper serial ports or internal modems. 1985 was when this revolution took place.

The same year saw an astonishing growth in the range of electronic services available for customers of all kinds; some represented substantial publishing activities, others allowed large companies to work ever more closely with their branches and men in the field or to communicate more effectively with retailers. The keen competition to sell new financial services made banks and building societies place even more of their future hopes in communications technology. At the same time the range of network facilities – the railway lines or roads along which data can travel from one remote location to another – has been considerably extended both in terms of sophistication and the number of people who expect to use it.

Finally, 1985 was an interesting year for hackers. It was when they became a substantial news story. This was no less puzzling to me than to other veteran network adventurers. *The Hacker's Handbook* originally had quite modest expectations. It was written because, halfway through 1984, it had become apparent that there was a growing but minority interest in the subject. The same questions were coming up over and over again in magazines and hobbyist bulletin boards. Why not produce a book to satisfy this demand, the publishers and I asked ourselves. At the same time I and a number of other hackers were concerned to make sure that those who were going to play around with other people's machines understood the fundamental ethics of hacking and that, without being too pompous about it, I thought I could do in this book.

The majority of books published each year are not intended to become best sellers (incidentally, if you are sufficiently skilled and talented you *can* aim a book at the best-seller list and, with a some luck, succeed). *The Hacker's Handbook* was simply designed to do well in what was beginning to become an ailing section of overall publishing activity – computer books. Instead, it became an event itself. A fresh look at hacking must take account of heightened levels of interest in the subject.

The New Hacker's Handbook reflects all these changes that have occurred in 1985. The book is more than 20 per cent longer than its predecessor, despite the fact that some material from the first edition has had to be removed for legal reasons.

The aims remain the same. The book is an accessible introduction to the techniques of making a micro speak to the outside world, a rapid survey of the sorts of information and data out there waiting to be siphoned through a domestic machine and a scene setter for those seduced by the sport of hacking. It is *not* the last word in hacking. No such book could ever exist because new 'last words' are being uttered all the time; indeed, that is one of the many attractions of the sport.

The word 'hacker' is used in two different but associated ways: for some, a hacker is merely a computer enthusiast of any kind, one who loves working with the beasties for their own sake, as opposed to operating them in order to enrich a company or research project – or to play games.

This book uses the word in a more restricted sense: hacking is a recreational and educational sport; it consists of attempting to make unauthorized entry into computers and to explore what is there. The sport's aims and purposes have been widely misunderstood; most hackers are *not* interested in perpetrating massive frauds, modifying their personal banking, taxation and employment records or inducing one world superpower into inadvertently commencing Armageddon in the mistaken belief that another superpower is about to attack it.

Every hacker I have ever come across has been quite clear where the fun lies: it is in developing an understanding of a system and finally producing the skills and tools to defeat it. In the vast majority of cases the process of 'getting in' is much more satisfying than what is in the end discovered from the protected computer files. In this respect the hacker is the direct descendant of the phone phreaks of fifteen years ago; phone phreaking became interesting as intranation and international subscriber trunk dialling was introduced, but when the London-based phreak finally chained his way through to Hawaii he usually had no one there to speak to, except the local weather service or American Express office, to confirm that the desired target had indeed been hit. Interestingly enough, one of the earliest of the present generation of hackers, Susan Headley, only seventeen when she began her exploits in California in 1977, chose as her target the local phone company and, with the information extracted from her hacks, ran all over the telephone network. In one of the many interviews which she has given since, she has explained what attracted her: it was a sense of power. Orthodox computer designers have to be among the intellectual elite of our time; and here was a seventeen-year-old blonde, hitherto heavily into rock musicians, showing their work up. She 'retired' four years later when a boyfriend started developing schemes to shut down part of the phone system. Last heard of, after giving evidence to a committee of the US Congress, she was working on a 'government project'.

There is also a strong affinity with program copy-protection crunchers. As is well known, much commercial software for micros is sold in a form to prevent obvious casual copying, say by loading a cassette, cartridge or disk into memory and then executing a 'save' onto a fresh blank cassette or disk. Copy-protection devices vary greatly in their methodology and sophistication and there are those who, without any commercial desire, enjoy nothing so much as defeating them. Every computer buff has met at least one cruncher with a vast store of commercial programs, all of which have somehow had the protection removed – and perhaps the main title subtly altered to show the cruncher's technical skills – but which are then never actually *used* at all.

Perhaps I should tell you what you can reasonably expect from this handbook: hacking is an activity like few others – it is semi-legal, seldom encouraged and, in its full extent, so vast that no individual or group, short of an organization like GCHQ or NSA, could hope to grasp a fraction of the possibilities. So this is not one of those books with titles like *Games Programming with the 6502* from which, if the book is any good, you are any good, and given a bit of time and enthusiasm, you will emerge with some mastery of the subject matter.

The aim of this handbook is to give you some grasp of

methodology, help you develop the appropriate attitudes and skills, provide essential background and some reference material, and point you in the right directions for more knowledge. Up to a point each chapter may be read by itself; it is a handbook and I have made extensive use of appendices which contain material which will be of use long after the main body of the text has been read.

It is one of the characteristics of hacking anecdotes, like those relating to espionage exploits, that almost no one closely involved has much stake in the truth; victims want to describe damage as minimal and perpetrators like to paint themselves as heroes while carefully disguising sources and methods. In addition, journalists who cover such stories are not always sufficiently competent to write accurately or even to know when they are being hoodwinked. (A note for journalists: any hacker who offers to break into a system on demand is conning you – the most you can expect is a repeat performance for your benefit of what a hacker has previously succeeded in doing. Getting to the 'front page' of a service or network need not imply that everything within that service can be accessed. Being able to retrieve confidential information, perhaps credit ratings, does not mean that the hacker is also able to *alter* that data. Remember the first rule of good reporting: be sceptical.)

So far as possible, I have tried to verify each story that appears in these pages, but despite what magazine articles have sought to suggest, it is the case that hackers work in isolated groups. A book which came out shortly after mine was called *Out of the Inner Circle* and many people persist in the view that somewhere, rather like the Holy Grail, this Inner Circle of hackers of superhuman power actually exists. (To be fair to the author of the book, Bill Landreth, and his friends, their choice of name was deliberately a bit jokey). The truth is that, at various times, groups of people with similar interests do come together and produce serendipitous results. One such recent British example went, during 1984, under the name Penzance. Slightly disguised, some Penzance material appears in chapter 5. Penzance was a veritable hothouse of talent; its members perpetrated many of the headline-grabbing events of recent years. It has changed its name several times since and, looking at what remains of it, it is obvious that it is no longer the focal information exchange it once was. Some hackers have retired, others have moved on and new ones are arriving. The new hackers often don't know the old. I am never surprised when a completely new group suddenly emerges and pulls off some startling stunt. I do not mind admitting that my sources on some of the important hacks of recent years are more remote than I would like. In these cases my accounts are of events and methods which, in all the circumstances, I believe are true. I welcome notes of correction.

Experienced hackers may identify one or two curious gaps in the range of coverage or less than full explanations. You can chose any combination of the following explanations without causing me any worry: first, I may be ignorant and incompetent; second, much of the fun of hacking is making your own discoveries and I wouldn't want to spoil that; third, maybe there are a few areas which really are best left alone.

Most of the material is applicable to readers in all countries; however, the author is British and so are most of his experiences.

The pleasures of hacking are possible at almost any level of computer competence beyond that of rank beginner and with fairly minimal equipment. It is quite difficult to describe the joy of using the world's cheapest micro, some clever firmware, a home-brew acoustic coupler and find that, courtesy of a friendly remote PDP 11/70 or VAX, you can be playing with the fashionable multitasking operating system, Unix.

The assumptions I have made about you as a reader are that you own a modest personal computer, a modem and some communications software which you know, roughly, how to use. (If you are not confident yet, practise logging onto a few hobbyist bulletin boards). For more advanced hacking, better equipment helps; but, just as very tasty photographs can be taken with snapshot cameras, do not believe that the computer equivalent of a Hasselblad with a trolleyload of accessories is essential.

Since you may at this point be suspicious that I have vast technical resources at my disposal, let me describe the kit that was used for most of my network adventures. At the centre was a battered old Apple II+, its lid off most of the time to draw away the heat from the many boards cramming the expansion slots. I use an industry standard dot matrix printer, famous equally for the variety of type founts possible and the paper-handling path which regularly skews off. I have several large crammed boxes of software as I collect comms software in particular like a deranged philatelist, but I use one package almost exclusively. Modems – well at this point the set-up does become unconventional: by the phone point are jack sockets for BT 95A, BT 96A, BT 600 and a North American modular jack. Somewhere around I have two acoustic couplers, devices for plunging telephone handsets into so that the computer can talk down the line, at the operating speeds of 300/300 and 75/1200 respectively, and three heavy mushroom-coloured 'shoe-boxes' representing British Telecom modem technology of five or more years ago and operating at various speeds and combinations of duplex/half-duplex. Whereas the acoustic coupler connects my computer to the line by audio, the modem links up at electrical level and is more accurate and free from error. More recently I have upgraded to an IBM PC clone upon which I run PC-Talk, an excellent 'freeware' package I obtained for the cost of the disk upon which its recorded and I have now rationalized my modem collection down to two: a 'smart' modem utilizing the AMD7910 chip (see chapter 3 and Appendix V) and a second-hand 1200/1200 full-duplex machine. My equipment for radio hacking is described in chapter 9. I have access to other equipment in my work and through friends, but that's what I used most of the time. Behind me is my other important bit of kit: a filing cabinet. Hacking is *not* an activity confined to sitting at keyboards and watching screens. All good hackers retain formidable collections of articles, promotional material and documentation. Read on and you will see why.

1985 has been the year in which hackers have had to think carefully about the ethics of hacking. Up till then, hacking's elite nature, it seemed to many of us, provided sufficient control to prevent matters getting out of hand. However, the number of copies sold of the first *Hacker's Handbook* is evidence (though not, I think, the cause) that there are many more would-be hackers than I ever thought likely. This, if nothing else, persuades me that rather more should be said both about the morality of hacking and the legal position.

I personally have always been quite sure about how far I am prepared to go in pursuing the hacking sport. For me, hacking is not, and never has been, an all-consuming activity. It is simply a natural extension of my fascination with computers, networks and new developments in technology. I want to know and experience the new before anybody else. Popping into people's computers to see what they are doing has always seemed to me little different from viewing those same machines on an exhibition stand or at a 'proper' demonstration, except that, using my way, I can explore and test from the comfort of my own home. Breaking into areas where I am supposed to be forbidden has always been part of testing the capability of a machine and its operators. But causing damage, wilfully or inadvertently, has never been part of this. Hackers like me – and the majority are – *admire* the machines that are our targets.

Until very recently, therefore, it never occurred to me to issue lectures on hacker behaviour. However, the small incidence of electronic vandalism from the hacking fraternity cannot be ignored, and every hacker who boasts about his (or her) activities, in 'safe' environments like bulletin boards and computer clubs or more widely, should think carefully about the consequences. Although I have had some extraordinary letters from readers – one exhorted me to use my talents to investigate the links between Denis Thatcher and the Falklands Island Company – I am not aware that I or any other hacker has so far been approached by master criminals or terrorists. Nevertheless, I suppose we should be cautious. A group of US hackers, annoyed that a *Newsweek* journalist called Richard Sandaza had betrayed what they regarded as confidences in the course of writing articles about the bulletin-board movement, decided to exact revenge. They accessed credit information about him from the computer-based resources of TRW (see chapter 4) and then posted the details on bulletin boards across the country. Journalists do behave appallingly on occasion, but I think the hackers should have restrained themselves.

To those who argue that a hacker's handbook must be giving guidance to potential criminals, I have two things to say: first, few people object to the sports of clay-pigeon shooting or archery although rifles, pistols and crossbows have no 'real' purpose other than to kill things; just as such sports are valid and satisfying in themselves, so hacking is quite sufficiently fulfilling without wreaking damage or violating people's privacy. Second, real hacking is rather more difficult than is often shown in the movies and on TV.

The sport of hacking should only be indulged in by those who are aware that they may find themselves inadvertently in breach of aspects of the law. Hacking itself is not against the law; indeed, it would be quite difficult to provide a good legal definition. How, for example, do you separate the hacker from someone who has forgotten a legitimately-owned password and attempts to recall it by successive tries at the keyboard, or the type of hack that starts with a legitimate entry to a system but then is able to move beyond those areas where the computer owners intended users to travel because the system was badly set up? Certain hacker-related activities may be illegal – phone phreaks were prosecuted for theft of electricity and, by extension, hackers could be charged with theft of CPU time or connect time. There could also be theft of copyright material on a database service – though this is likely to be a civil rather than criminal matter. The amounts of money involved here are likely to be small. An hour's illegal use of even the most highly priced database service would cost, at usual rates, just over £100 – not a large crime by most standards. There is also the suggestion that use of an illegitimately acquired password could amount to uttering a forgery; the ingredients of this criminal charge are that there must be some article which is forged – it could be an electronic disk – and someone who was misled in some way as a result. Any damage deliberately caused would be regarded as criminal damage. Hackers of the radio waves should be aware of the Wireless Telegraphy Act, the Telecommunications Act and the Interception of Communications Act. Nevertheless, there are plenty of types of hacking which do not appear to be illegal.

If you hack into a database containing personal information, you may be the cause of getting the database *owner* into trouble. Under the Data Protection Act, 1985, and the many similar worldwide items of legislation, the database owner now has a duty to prevent unauthorized disclosure and has to pay compensation to those individuals whose details he has allowed to leak out.

It may be special pleading but I believe that too much effort for too little result is currently being expended by the authorities in trying to prosecute hackers. Most hacking offences are of the same order of moral turpitude as parking on double yellow lines. The substantive damage some recent hacks have caused has been to the credibility of the victims – and sometimes those victims have made the damage worse by ostentatiously drawing attention to it. In fact, real computer fraud is exceptionally difficult to investigate and even more difficult to bring to the courts because of sheer technical complexity; chasing hackers gives the authorities the illusion that they are doing something about computer crime, of which hacking is such a small part both in absolute numbers and in terms of the money involved. But if you are a hacker, be careful – to be the object of a prosecution, even an unsuccessful one, may be much more than you are willing to pay for a minor hobby.

As with the original book, various people helped me on various aspects of this book; they must all remain unnamed – they know who they are and that they have my thanks.

1 First Principles

The first hack I ever did was executed at an exhibition stand run by British Telecom's then rather new Prestel service. Earlier, in an adjacent conference hall, an enthusiastic speaker had demonstrated viewdata's potential worldwide spread by logging onto Viditel, the infant Dutch service. He had had, as so often happens in the these circumstances, difficulty in logging on first time. He was using one of those sets that displays auto-dialled telephone numbers so that was how I found the number to call. By the time he had finished his third unsuccessful log-on attempt I (and presumably several others) had all the pass numbers. While the BT staff were busy with other visitors to their stand, I picked out for myself a relatively neglected viewdata set. I knew that it was possible to bypass the auto-dialler with its preprogrammed phone numbers in this particular model simply by picking up the the phone adjacent to it, dialling my preferred number, waiting for the whistle, and then hitting the keyboard button labelled 'viewdata'. I dialled Holland, performed my little bypass trick and watched Viditel write itself on the screen. The pass numbers were accepted first time and, courtesy of ... no, I'll spare them embarrassment ... I had only lack of fluency in Dutch to restrain my explorations. Fortunately the first BT executive to spot what I had done was amused as well.

Most hackers seem to have started in a similar way. Essentially you rely on the foolishness and inadequate sense of security of computer salesman, operators, programmers and designers.

For a number of years I was a hacker without realizing it. My original basic motive was that I wanted to look at remote databases without having a salesperson guiding my fingers. A skilled demonstrator can dazzle you with flashy features and stop you seeing how limited or clumsy the service actually is. Many people would have thought my level of interest rather technical: I wanted to see how quickly the remote computer responded to my requests, how easy the instructions were to follow, how complete the information and facilities offered. I have always been seduced by the vision of the universal electronic information service and I wanted to be among the first to use it.

So I began to collect phone numbers and passwords; when I didn't have a legitimate password I 'invented' or discovered one. I thought of these episodes as country walks across a landscape of computer networks. The owners of these services, by and large, were anxious to acquire customers and, so I told myself, rather like farmers who don't mind careful ramblers, polite network adventurers like me were tolerated. After all, if I liked a service I would be likely to talk about it to potential customers.

In the early days of the computer clubs, the sort that met after hours in the local polytechnic, I began to find people who had similarly acquired lists of interesting phone numbers, only their preoccupations were not always the same as mine. There were those who sought facilities for playing with advanced languages of the type that could not be placed on micros, and those who wanted to locate the 'big' games that had to live on big machines if they were to run.

It wasn't really until late 1982 that anyone I knew used the word 'hacker' in its modern context. Up till then hackers were American computer buffs who messed around on mainframes or had built their own home computers in garages. Quite suddenly, no one knew where from, 'hacker' had a new and specific meaning. At about the same time it became evident that there were network explorers whose main interest was not the remote computers themselves but the defeat of entry validation procedures.

Then came the bulletin boards, and with them the hacker's SIGs (special interest groups), and for the first time I became aware just how many people seemed to have acquired the same curious interests as I had.

In the introduction to this book I refer to the pursuit as a sport and, like most sports, it is both relatively pointless and filled with rules, written or otherwise, which have to be obeyed if there is to be any meaningfulness placed on the activity. Just as rugby football is not just about forcing a ball down one end of a field, so hacking is not just about using any means to secure access to a computer. On this basis opening private correspondence to secure a password on a public access service like Prestel and then running around the system building up someone's bill is not what hackers call hacking. The critical element must be the use of skill in some shape or form.

Contrary to what is often thought, hacking is not a new pursuit. I was certainly no pioneer. It started in the early 1960s when the first 'serious' time-share computers started to appear at university sites. Very early on 'unofficial' areas of the memory started to appear, first as mere noticeboards and scratchpads for private programming experiments, then as locations for games. Where and how do you think the early Space Invaders, Lunar Landers and Adventure Games were created? Perhaps tech-hacking – the mischievous manipulation of technology – goes back even farther. One of the old favourites of US campus life was to rewire the control panels of elevators (lifts) in high-rise buildings, so that a request for the third floor resulted in the occupants being whizzed to the twenty-third.

Towards the end of the sixties, when the first experimental networks arrived on the scene, particularly the legendary ARPAnet (Advanced Research Projects Agency network), the computer hackers skipped out of their own local computers, along the packet-switched high-grade communications lines, and into the other machines on the net.

But all these hackers were privileged individuals – they were at a university or research resource, and they were able to borrow terminals to work with. What has changed now, of course, is the wide availability of home computers – and the modems to go with them, the growth of public-access networking of computers, and the enormous quantity and variety of computers that can be accessed.

Hackers vary considerably in their native computer skills. A basic knowledge of how data is held on computers and can be transferred from one to another is essential; determination, alertness, opportunism, the abilities to analyse and synthesise, the collecting of relevant helpful data and luck – the pre-requisites of any intelligence officer – are equally important. If you can write quick effective programs in either a high-level language or machine code, well, it helps. A knowledge of on-line query procedures is helpful and the ability to work in one or more popular mainframe and mini operating systems could put you in the big league.

The material and information you need to hack are all around you, only they are seldom marked as such. Remember that a large proportion of what is passed off as 'secret intelligence' is openly available, if only you know where to look and appreciate what you find.

At one time or another, hacking will test everything you know about computers and communications. You will discover your abilities increase in fits and starts and you must be prepared for long periods when nothing new appears to happen.

Popular films and TV series have built up a mythology of what hackers can do and with what degree of ease. My personal delight in such dream factory output is in compiling a list of all the mistakes in each such episode. Anyone who has ever tried to move a graphics game from one micro to an almost similar competitor will know already that the chances of getting a home micro to display the North Atlantic strategic situation as it would be viewed from the President's command post are slim even if appropriate telephone numbers and passwords were available. Less immediately obvious is the fact that most home micros talk to the outside world through limited but convenient asynchronous protocols, effectively denying direct access to the mainframe products of the world's undisputed leading computer manufacturer, which favours synchronous protocols. And home micro displays are memory-mapped, not vector-traced, etc.

Nevertheless it is astonishingly easy to get remarkable results – and, thanks to the protocol-transformation facilities of PADs in PSS networks (of which much more later), you *can* get into large IBM devices.

The cheapest hacking kit I have ever used consisted of a ZX81, 16 K RAM pack, a clever firmware accessory and an acoustic coupler. Total cost, just over £100. The ZX81's touch-membrane keyboard was one liability, so were the uncertainties of the various connectors. Much of the cleverness of the firmware was devoted to overcoming the native drawbacks of the ZX81's inner configuration – the fact that it didn't readily send and receive characters in the industry-standard ASCII code, and that the output port was designed more for instant access to the Z80's main logic rather than to use industry-standard serial port protocols and to rectify the limited screen display.

Yet this kit was capable of adjusting to most bulletin boards; could get into most dial-up 300/300 asynchronous ports, reconfiguring for word length and parity if needed; could have accessed a PSS PAD and hence got into a huge range of computers not normally available to microowners; and, with another modem, could have got into viewdata services. You could print out pages on the ZX 'tinfoil' printer.

The disadvantages of this kit were all in convenience, not in facilities. Chapter 3 describes the sort of kit most hackers use.

It is even possible to hack with no equipment at all; all major banks now have a network of 'hole in the wall' cash machines – ATMs or automatic teller machines, as they are officially known. Major building societies have their own network. These machines have had faults in software design, and the hackers who played around with them used no more equipment than their fingers and brains. More about this later.

Although I have no intention of writing at length about hacking etiquette, it is worth one paragraph: lovers of fresh-air walks obey the Country Code, involving such items as closing gates behind them and avoiding damage to crops and livestock. Something very similar ought to guide your rambles into other people's computers: don't manipulate files unless you are sure a back-up exists; don't crash operating systems; don't lock legitimate users out from access; watch who you give information to; if you really discover something confidential, keep it to yourself. In fact, think carefully who you tell about *any* hacking success. Hacking itself rarely causes much *direct* damage; however, publicity can cause the hacked computer's owners to suffer severe loss in credibility. Talking to journalists, particularly those on the national press, may be appealing to the immature hacker's ego but the real damage an oversensationalized account of your exploits can cause should never be underestimated. It should go without saying that hackers are not interested in fraud. Finally, just as any rambler who ventures across a field guarded by barbed wire and dotted with notices warning about the Official Secrets Acts would deserve most that happened thereafter, there are a few hacking projects which should never be attempted.

On the converse side, I and many hackers I know are convinced of one thing: we receive more than a little help from the system managers of the computers we attack. In the case of computers owned by universities and polys, there is little doubt that a number of them are viewed like academic libraries – strictly speaking they are for the student population, but if outsiders seriously thirsty for knowledge show up, they aren't turned away. As for other computers, a number of us are almost sure we have been used as a cheap means to test a system's defences ... someone releases a phone number and low-level password to hackers (there are plenty of ways) and watches what happens over the next few weeks while the computer files themselves are empty of sensitive data. Then, when the results have been noted, the phone numbers and passwords are changed, the security improved, and so on – much easier on dp budgets than employing programmers at £150/man/day or more. Certainly the Pentagon has been known to form 'Tiger Units' of US Army computer specialists to pinpoint weaknesses in systems security.

Two spectacular hacks of recent years have captured the public imagination: the first, the Great Prince Philip Prestel Hack, which, as this edition is being prepared, is the subject of unresolved criminal charges and cannot really be described or discussed at this time, although from every point of view – technical, social and legal – hacking history is likely to regard it as 'important'. The second was spectacular because it was carried out on live national television. It occurred on 2 October 1983 during a follow-up to the BBC's successful 'Computer Literacy' series. It is worth reporting here, because it neatly illustrates the essence of hacking as a sport – skill with systems, careful research, maximum impact with minimum real harm, and humour.

The TV presenter, John Coll, was trying to show off the Telecom Gold electronic mail service. Coll had hitherto never liked long passwords and, in the context of the tight timing and pressures of live TV, a two-letter password seemed a good idea at the time. On Telecom Gold it is only the password that is truly confidential; system and account numbers, as well as phone numbers to log onto the system, are easily obtainable. The BBC's account number, extensively publicized, was OWL001, the owl being the logo for the TV series as well as the BBC computer.

The hacker, who appeared on a subsequent programme as a 'former hacker', and who talked about his activities in general but did not openly acknowledge his responsibility for the BBC act, managed to seize control of Coll's mailbox and superimpose a message of his own:

Computer Security Error. Illegal access. I hope your television PROGRAMME runs as smoothly as my PROGRAM worked out your passwords! Nothing is secure!

Hackers' Song

Put another password in,
Bomb it out and try again
Try to get past logging in,
We're hacking, hacking, hacking.

Try his first wife's maiden name,
This is more than just a game,
It's real fun, but just the same,
It's hacking, hacking, hacking.

The Nutcracker (Hackers UK)

HI THERE, OWLETS, FROM OZ AND YUG (OLIVER AND GUY)

After the hack a number of stories about how it had been carried out, and by whom, circulated. It was suggested that the hackers had crashed through to the operating system of the Prime computers upon which the Dialcom electronic mail software resided. It was also suggested that the BBC had arranged the whole thing as a stunt, or, alternatively, that some BBC employees had fixed it up without telling their colleagues. Getting to the truth of a legend in such cases is almost always impossible. No one involved has a stake in the truth. British Telecom, with a strong commitment to get Gold accepted in the business community, was anxious to suggest that only the dirtiest of dirty tricks could remove the inherent confidentiality of their electronic mail service. Naturally the British Broadcasting Corporation rejected any possibility that it would connive in an irresponsible cheap stunt. But the hacker had no great stake in the truth either – he had sources and contacts to protect and his image in the hacker community to bolster. Never expect *any* hacking anecdote to be completely truthful.

2 Computer-to-Computer Communications

Services intended for access by microcomputers are nowadays usually presented in a very user-friendly fashion: pop in your software disk or firmware, check the connections, dial the telephone number, listen for the tone ... and there you are. Hackers, interested in venturing where they are not invited, enjoy no such luxury. They may want to access older services which preceded the modern 'human interface'; they are very likely to travel along paths intended not for ordinary customers but for engineers or salesmen; they could be utilizing facilities that were part of a computer's commissioning process and have been hardly used since.

So the hacker needs a greater knowledge of data-comms technology than more passive computer users and, because of its growth pattern and the fact that many interesting installations still use yesterday's solutions, some feeling for the history of the technology is pretty essential.

Getting one computer to talk to another some distance away means accepting a number of limiting factors:

1 Although computers can send out several bits of information at once, the ribbon cable necessary to do this is not economical at any great length, particularly if the information is to be sent out over a network. Each wire in the ribbon would need switching separately, thus making exchanges prohibitively expensive. So bits must be transmitted one at at time, or serially.
2 Since you will be using, in the first instance, wires and networks already installed – in the form of the telephone and telex networks – you must accept that the limited bandwidth of these facilities will restrict the rate at which data can be sent. The data will pass through long lengths of wire, frequently being reamplified, undergoing degradation as it passes through dirty

switches and relays in a multiplicity of exchanges.
3 Data must be easily capable of accurate recovery at the far end.
4 Sending and receiving computers must be synchronized in their working.
5 The mode in which data is transmitted must be one understood by all computers; accepting a standard protocol may mean adopting the speed and efficiency of the slowest.

The present 'universal' standard for data transmission, as used by microcomputers and many other services, uses agreed tones to signify binary 0 and binary 1, the ASCII character set (also known as International Alphabet No. 5), and an asynchronous protocol whereby the transmitting computer and the receiving computer are locked in step every time a character is sent and not just at the beginning of a transmission stream. Like nearly all standards, it is highly arbitrary in its decisions and derives its importance simply from the fact of being generally accepted. Like many standards too, there are a number of subtle and important variations.

To see how the standard works, how it came about and the reasons for the variations, we need to look back a little into history.

The Growth of Telegraphy

The essential techniques of sending data along wires has a history of 150 years, and some of the common terminology of modern data transmission goes right back to the first experiments.

The earliest form of telegraphy, itself the earliest form of electrical message sending, used the remote actuation of electrical relays to leave marks on a strip of paper. The letters of the alphabet were defined by the patterns of 'mark' and 'space'. The terms have come through to the present, to signify binary conditions of '1' and '0' respectively. The first reliable machine for sending letters and figures by this method dates from 1840. The direct successor of that machine, using remarkably unchanged electromechanical technology and a 5-bit alphabetic code, is still in wide use today, as the telex/teleprinter/teletype. The mark and space have been replaced by holes punched in paper tape, larger holes for mark, smaller ones for space. The code is called Baudot, after its inventor. Synchronization between sending and receiving stations is carried out by beginning each *letter* with a 'start' bit (a space) and concluding it with a 'stop' bit (mark). The 'idle' state of a circuit is thus 'mark'. In effect, therefore, each letter requires the transmission of 7 bits:

. * * . . . * (letter A: . = space; * = mark)

of which the first . is the start bit, the last * is the stop bit and * * . . . is the code for A.

It is the principal means of sending text messages around the world and the way in which news reports are distributed globally. And, until Third World countries are rich enough to afford more advanced devices, the technology will survive.

Early Computer Communications
When, 110 years after the first such machines came on line, the need arose to address computers remotely, telegraphy was the obvious way to do so. No one expected computers in the early 1950s to give instant results; jobs were assembled in batches, often fed in by means of paper tape (another borrowing from telex, still in use), and then run. The instant calculation and collation of data was then considered quite miraculous. So the first use of data communications was almost exclusively to ensure that the machine was fed with up-to-date information, not for the machine to send the results out to those who might want it; they could wait for the 'printout' in due course, borne to them with considerable solemnity by the computer experts. Typical communications speeds were 50 or 75 bits/s. (It is here we must introduce the distinction between bits/s and baud rate, which many people who ought to know better seem to believe are one and the same thing. The baud is the measure of speed of data transmission; specifically, it refers to the number of signal level changes per second. At lower speeds bits/s and baud rate are identical, but at higher speeds bits are communicated by methods other than varying the signal level, typically by detection of the phase state of a signal. Thus, 1200 bits/s full duplex is actually achieved by a 600-baud signal using four phase angles. We'll examine this later.)

These early computers were, of course, in today's jargon, single-user/single-task; programs were fed by direct machine coding. Gradually, over the next fifteen years, computers spawned multi-user capabilities by means of time-sharing techniques and their human interface became more 'user-friendly'. With these facilities grew the demand for remote access to computers and modern data communications began.

Even at the very end of the 1960s, when I had my own very first encounter with a computer, the links with telegraphy were still obvious. As a result of happenstance I was in a government-run research facility to the southwest of London and the program I was to use was located on a computer just to the north of Central London; I was sat down in front of a battered teletype – capitals and figures only, and requiring not inconsiderable physical force from my smallish fingers to actuate the keys of my choice. Being a teletype and outputting onto a paper roll, mistakes could not as readily be erased as on a VDU, and since the sole form of error reporting consisted of a solitary '?', the episode was more frustrating than thrilling. VDUs and good keyboards were then far too expensive for 'ordinary' use.

The Telephone Network
But by that time all sorts of changes in data-comms were taking place. The telex and telegraphy network, originally so important, had long been overtaken by voice-grade telephone circuits (Bell's invention dates from 1876). For computer communication, mark and space could be indicated by different audio tones rather than by different voltage conditions. Data traffic on a a telex line can only operate in one direction at a time, but by selecting different pairs of tones both 'transmitter' and 'receiver' can speak simultaneously – so that, in fact, one has to talk about 'originate' and 'answer' instead.

Improved electrical circuit design meant that higher speeds than 50 or 75 bits/s became possible; there was a move to 110 bits/s, then 300 and, so far as ordinary telephone circuits are concerned, 2400 bits/s is now regarded as the top limit. Special techniques are required to achieve this speed.

The 'start' and 'stop' method of synchronizing the near and far end of a communications circuit at the beginning of each individual letter has been retained, but the common use of the 5-bit Baudot code has been replaced by a 7-bit extended code which allows for many more characters, 128 in fact.

Lastly, to reduce errors in transmission due to noise in the telephone line and circuitry, each letter can be checked by the use of a further bit (the parity bit), which adds up all the bits in the main character and then, depending on whether the result is odd or even, adds a binary 0 or binary 1.

The full modern transmission of a letter in this system, in this case K, therefore, looks like this:

START-STOP TRANSMISSION OF A DATA CHARACTER

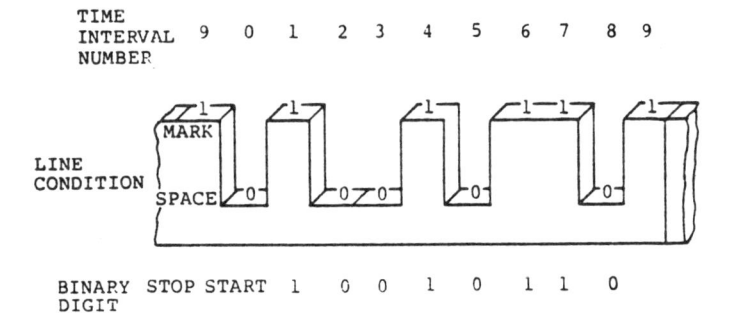

```
TIME
INTERVAL   9   0   1   2   3   4   5   6   7   8   9
NUMBER
```

LINE CONDITION: MARK (1) / SPACE (0)

```
BINARY    STOP START  1   0   0   1   0   1   1   0
DIGIT
```

The first 0 is the start bit; then follow 7 bits of the actual letter code (1001011); then the parity bit; then the final 1 is the stop code.

This system, asynchronous start-stop, ASCII (the common name for the alphabetic code), is the basis for nearly all micro-based communications. The key variations relate to:

bit-length: you can have 7 or 8 databits.*

parity: it can be even or odd, or entirely absent.*

tones: the tones used to signify binary 0 and binary 1, and which computer is in 'originate' and which in 'answer', can vary according to the speed of the transmission and also according to whether the service is used in North America or the rest of the world. Briefly, most of the world uses tones and standards laid down by the Geneva-based organization CCITT, a specialized agency of the International Telecommunications Union; whereas in the United

---

* There are no 'obvious explanations' for the variations commonly found: most electronic mail services and viewdata transmit 7 data bits, even parity and 1 stop bit; Telecom Gold and most hobbyist bulletin boards transmit 8 data bits, no parity and 1 stop bit. Most systems which use 7 bits, 1 stop bit, even parity, work just as well on 8 bits, 1 stop bit, no parity. These variants are sometimes written in a shorthand form: '7e1' means '7 bits, even parity, 1 stop bit' '8n1' means '8 bits, no parity, 1 stop bit' and so on. 7-bit transmission will cover most forms of text matter, but if you wish to send machine code or other program material, or text prepared with a wordprocessor like Wordstar which uses hidden codes for formatting, then you must use 8-bit transmission protocols. Terminal emulator software – see chapter 3 – allows users to adjust for these differing requirements.

States and most parts of Canada, tones determined by the telephone utility, colloquially known as Ma Bell, are adopted.

The following table gives the standards and tones in common use.

Service designator	Speed	Duplex	Transmit 0	Transmit 1	Receive 0	Receive 1	Answer
V.21 orig	300*	full	1180	980	1850	1650	–
V.21 ans	300*	full	1850	1650	1180	980	2100
V.23 (1)	600	half	1700	1300	1700	1300	2100
V.23 (2)	1200	f/h†	2100	1300	2100	1300	2100
V.23 back	75	f/h†	450	390	450	390	–
Bell 103 orig	300*	full	1070	1270	2025	2225	–
Bell 103 ans	300*	full	2025	2225	1070	1270	2225
Bell 202	1200	half	2200	1200	2200	1200	2025
V.22/212A	1200	full			(see below)		
V.22 bis	2400	full			(see below)		

* Any speed up to 300 bits/s can also include 75 and 110 bits/s services.

† Service can either be half duplex at 1200 bits/s or asymmetrical full duplex, with 75 bits/s originate and 1200 bits/s receive (commonly used as viewdata user) or 1200 transmit and 75 receive (viewdata host).

Higher Speeds

1200 bits/s is usually regarded as the fastest speed possible on an ordinary voice-grade telephone line. Beyond this, noise on the line due to the switching circuits at the various telephone exchanges, poor cabling, etc., make accurate transmission difficult. However, 2400 bits/s is becoming more common and, indeed, is the standard speed of teletex, the high-speed version of telex.

Transmission at these higher speeds uses different signalling techniques from those hitherto described. Simple tone detection circuits cannot switch on and off sufficiently rapidly to be reliable, so another method of detecting individual 'bits' has to be employed. The way it is done is by using *phase detection*. The rate of signalling doesn't go up – it stays at 600 baud – but each signal is modulated at origin by phase and then demodulated in the same way at the far end. Two channels are used, high and low (what else), so that you can achieve bi-directional or duplex communication.

The tones are:

originate (low channel) 1200 Hz
answer (high channel) 2400 Hz

and they are the same for the European CCITT V.22 standard and for the Bell equivalent, Bell 212A. V.22 bis is the variant for 2400 bits/s full-duplex transmission; there is no equivalent Bell term.

The speed differences are obtained in this way:

600 bits/s (V.22) Each bit encoded as a phase change from the previous phase. There are two possible symbols which consist of one of two phase angles; each symbol conveys 1 bit of information.
1200 bits/s (V.22 and Bell 212A) Differential phase shift keying is used to give four possible symbols which consist of one of four phase angles. Each symbol coveys 2 bits of information to enable a 600-baud signal rate to handle 1200 bits.
2400 bits/s (V.22 bis) Quadrature amplitude modulation is used to give 16 possible symbols which consist of twelve phase angles and three levels of amplitude. Each symbol conveys 4 bits of information to enable a 600-baud signal rate to handle 2400 bits.

It is the requirement for much more sophisticated modulation and demodulation techniques that has up till now kept higher-speed modems out of the hands of home enthusiasts, because of cost.

Where higher speeds are required, leased circuits, not available via dial-up, become essential. The leased circuit is paid for on a fixed charge, not a charge based on time connected. Such circuits can be 'conditioned', by using special amplifiers, etc., to support the higher data rate.

For really high-speed transmissions, however, pairs of copper cable are inadequate. Medium speed is obtainable by the use of coaxial cable (a little like that used for TV antenna hook-ups) which have a very broad bandwidth. Imposing several different channels on one cable length is called multiplexing and, depending on the application, the various channels can either carry several different computer conversations simultaneously or can send several bits of one computer conversation in parallel, just as though there were a ribbon cable between the two participating computers. Either way, what happens is that each binary 0 or binary 1 is given not an audio tone but a radio-frequency tone.

Error Correction
At higher speeds it becomes increasingly important to use transmission protocols that include error correction. Error-correction techniques usually consist of dividing the transmission stream into a series of blocks which can be checked, one at a time, by the receiving computer. The 'parity' system mentioned above is one example, but obviously a crude one. The difficulty is that the more secure an error-correction protocol becomes, the greater the overhead in terms of numbers of bits transmitted to send just one character from one computer to another. Thus, in the typical 300 bit situation, the actual letter is defined by 7 bits, 'start' and 'stop' account for another 2, and the check takes a further 1 – 10 in all. After a while, what you gain in the speed with which each actual *bit* is transmitted you lose because so many bits have to be sent to ensure that a single *character* is accurately received!

Parity checking has its limitations: it will pick up only one error per character; if there are two or more then the error gets 'printed'; in other words, an inaccurate character is received as valid. There are a large number of error-correction protocols, although, as mentioned above, the principle is nearly always the same: the originating computer divides the character stream to be sent into a series of blocks, say 128 bits or alternative base 8 or base 16 figure. The value of each bit in the block is then put through a short mathematical process (typically, adding) and the result, known as a 'checksum', is placed at the end of the block. The block is then sent down the line. The receiving computer accepts the 128 bits and the checksum and stores them in a temporary buffer; here the mathematical process is quickly repeated. If the addition (or whatever) agrees with the checksum, the 128 bits are released to the receiving computer's user and a quick acknowledgement of correct reception is sent back to the originating computer, which then prepares the next block, and so on until the entire file has been sent. If the receiving computer gets a garbled block, then it is retransmitted as necessary.

So much for the principles; unfortunately there are a large number of implementations of this basic idea. The variations depend on: size of block transmitted, checksum method, form of acknowledgement, and number of unsuccessful tries permitted before transmission is aborted. Here are some of the more common error-correction protocols:

ARQ This is often implemented in *hardware* in 1200 full-duplex modems. Sending and receiving computers use no error correction protocol, but the modems, one at each end, introduce error correction 'transparently', in other words, they take care of the checking without either of the computers being aware of what is happening.

Xmodem (sometimes called Christiansen, after its deviser.) This protocol started out among hobbyists who wished to transfer files between one another. Christiansen made his software public domain, so that users didn't have to pay for its use, and this has contributed to its popularity. Xmodem is often to be found on bulletin boards and versions have been implemented for most of the popular families of computers like C/PM and MSDOS. You may have difficulty in getting a copy if your computer was primarily for the 'home' market and does not run one of the well-known operating systems. There are two variants of Xmodem, the more recent of which has an option giving a higher degree of protection using CRC – cyclical redundancy checking – so be warned!

Kermit This has the distinction of being implemented on more computers, particularly mainframes, than any other. It was devised at Columbia University, New York, and the only micros that appear to have easily available versions are the IBM PC, Apple and CP/M. Contact the user groups for copies which are free, although you will have to pay for the disk media. Among the big machines that carry Kermit are DEC 10s and 20s, DEC VAX and PDP 11 and the IBM 370 series under VM and CMS.

CET Telesoftware This is to be found on videotex (viewdata) systems (see chapter 8 for more) and is used to transfer programs in the videotex page format. The checksum is based on the entire videotex page and not on small blocks. This is because the smallest element a videotex host can retransmit is an entire page. This is one of the features that makes telesoftware downloading rather tiresome – one slight error and over 8 kbits must be retransmitted each time at 1200 bits/s! And the retransmission request goes back to the host at only 75 bits/s!

EPAD EPAD is used in connection with packet-switched services (see chapter 7). If you have an ordinary micro and wish to use a service operating on PSS, you must dial into a device called a PAD (packet assembler/disassembler), which transforms material from your machine into the packets required for the packet-switching service, and vice versa. The trouble is that, while PSS and its cousins use error correction during their high-speed international journeys, until recently there was no error correction between the PAD and the end-user's computer. EPAD was introduced to overcome this difficulty.

There are many many other error-correction protocols. A number of the (rather expensive) terminal emulator software packages available for micros have their own proprietary products – Crosstalk, BSTAM, Move-It, Datasoft are all different. They all work, but only when computers at both ends of the transmission line are using them.

Synchronous Protocols
In the asynchronous protocols so far described, transmitting and receiving computers are kept in step with each other every time a character is sent, via the 'start' and 'stop' bits. In synchronous comms, the locking together is done merely at the start of each block of transmission by the sending of a special code (often SYN). The SYN code starts a clock (a timed train of pulses) in the receiver and it is this that ensures that binary 0s and 1s originating at the transmitter are correctly interpreted by the receiver. Clearly the displacement of even one binary digit can cause havoc.

A variety of synchronous protocols exist – the length of block sent each time, the form of checking that takes place, the form of acknowledgement, and so on. A synchronous protocol is not only a function of the modem, which has to have a suitable clock, but also of the software and firmware in the computers. Because asynchronous protocols transmit so many 'extra' bits in order to avoid error, savings in transmission time under synchronous systems often exceed 20-30 per cent. The disadvantage of synchronous protocols lies in increased hardware costs. Error correction is built into synchronous protocols.

One other complication exists: most asynchronous protocols use the ASCII code to define characters. IBM (Big Blue), the biggest enthusiast of synchronous comms, has its own binary code to define characters. In appendix IV, you will find an explanation and a comparison with ASCII.

The best-known IBM protocol which is sent along phone lines is BSC; other IBM protocols use coaxial cable between terminal and mainframe. The hacker, wishing to come to terms with synchronous comms, has two choices. The more expensive is to purchase a protocol converter board. These are principally available for the IBM PC, which has been increasingly marketed for the 'executive workstation' audience where the ability to interface to a company's existing (IBM) mainframe is a key feature. The alternative is to see whether the target mainframe has a port onto a packet-switched service; in that event the hacker can use ordinary asynchronous equipment and protocols – the local PAD will carry out the necessary transformations.

Networks
Which brings us neatly to the world of high-speed digital networks using packet switching. All the computer communications so far described have taken place either on the phone (voice-grade) network or on the telex network. In chapter 7 we look at packet switching and the opportunities offered by international data networks.

We must now specify hackers' equipment in more detail.

3 Hackers' Equipment

You can hack with almost any microcomputer capable of talking to the outside world via a serial port and a modem. In fact, you don't even need a micro; my first hack was with a perfectly ordinary viewdata terminal.

What follows in this chapter, therefore, is a description of the elements of a system I like to think of as optimum for straightforward asynchronous ASCII and Baudot communications. What is at issue is convenience as much as anything. With kit like this you will be able to get through most dial-up ports and into packet switching through a PAD (packet assembler/disassembler) port. It will not get you into IBM networks because these use different and incompatible protocols; we will return to the matter of the IBM world in chapter 10. In other words, given a bit of money, a bit of knowledge, a bit of help from friends and a bit of luck, what is described is the sort of equipment most hackers have at their command.

You will find few products on the market labelled 'for hackers'; you must select those items which appear to have 'legitimate' but interesting functions and see if they can be bent to the hacker's purposes. The various sections within this chapter highlight the sort of facilities you need; before lashing out on some new software or hardware, try to get hold of as much publicity and documentation material as possible to see how adaptable the products are. In a few cases it is worth looking at the secondhand market, particularly for modems, cables and test equipment.

Although it is by no means essential, an ability to solder a few connections and scrabble among the circuit diagrams of 'official' products often yields unexpectedly rewarding results.

The Computer
Almost any popular microcomputer will do; hacking does not call upon enormous reserves of computer power. Nearly everything you hack will come to you in alphanumeric form, not graphics. The computer you already have will almost certainly have the essential qualities. However the very cheapest micros, like the ZX81, while usable, require much more work on the part of the

operator/hacker and give him far less in the way of instant facilities. (In fact, as the ZX81 doesn't use ASCII internally, but a Sinclair-developed variant, you will need a software or firmware fix for that, before you even think of hooking it up to a modem.)

Most professional data services assume the user is viewing on an eighty-column screen; ideally the hacker's computer should be capable of doing that as well, otherwise the display will be full of awkward line breaks. Terminal emulator software (see below) can sometimes provide a 'fix'.

One or two disk drives are pretty helpful, because you will want to be able to save the results of your network adventures as quickly and efficiently as possible. Most terminal emulators use the computer's free memory (i.e. all that not required to support operating system and the emulator software itself) as store for the received data, but once the buffer is full, you will begin to lose the earliest items. You can, of course, try to save to cassette, but normally that is a slow and tedious process.

An alternative storage method is to save to a printer, printing the received data stream not only to the computer screen, but also on a dot-matrix printer. However, most of the more popular (and cheaper) printers do not work sufficiently fast. You may find you lose characters at the beginning of each line. Moreover, if you print everything in real time, you'll include all your mistakes, false starts etc., and in the process use masses of paper. So if you can save to disk regularly, you can review each hack afterwards at your leisure and, using a screen editor or word processor, save or print out only those items of real interest.

The computer must have a serial port, either called that or marked RS232C (or its slight variant RS434) or V.24, which is the official designator of RS232C used outside the USA, although not often seen on micros.

Serial Ports
The very cheapest micros, like the ZX81, Spectrum or VIC20, do not have RS232C ports, though add-on boards are available. Some of the older personal computers, like the Apple, the original Pet, etc., were also originally sold without serial ports, although standard boards are available for all of these.

You are probably aware that the RS232C standard has a large number of variants and that not all computers (or add-on boards) that claim to have a RS232C port can actually talk into a modem.

Historically, RS232C/V.24 is supposed to cover all aspects of serial communication and includes printers and dumb terminals as well as computers. The RS232C standard specifies electrical and physical requirements. Everything is pumped through a 25-pin D-shaped connector, each pin of which has some function in some implementation. But in most cases nearly all the pins are ignored. In practice only three connections are absolutely essential for computer-to-modem communication:

pin 7   signal ground

pin 2   characters leaving the computer

pin 3   characters arriving at the computer

The remaining connections are for such purposes as feeding power to an external device, switching the external device on or off, exchanging status and timing signals, monitoring the state of the line, etc. Some computers, their associated firmware and particular software packages, require one or other of these status signals to go 'high' or 'low' in particular circumstances, or the program hangs. On the IBM PC, for example, pin 5 (clear to send), pin 6 (data set ready) and pin 20 (data terminal ready) are often all used. If you are using an auto-answer modem – one which will intercept an inward phone call automatically – then you must also have a properly functioning pin 22 (ring indicator). Check your documentation if you have trouble. A fuller explanation of RS232C appears in appendix VI.

Some RS232C implementations on microcomputers or add-on boards are there simply to support printers with serial interfaces, but they can often be modified to talk into modems. The critical two lines are those serving pins 2 and 3.

A computer serving a modem needs a cable in which pin 2 on the computer is linked to pin 2 on the modem.

A computer serving a printer, etc., needs a cable in which pin 3 on the computer is linked to pin 2 on the printer and pin 3 on the printer is linked to pin 2 on the computer.

If two computers are linked together directly, without a modem, then pin 2 on computer A must be linked to pin 3 on computer B, and pin 3 on computer B linked to pin 2 on computer A. This arrangement is sometimes called a 'null modem' or a 'null modem cable'.

There are historical 'explanations' for these arrangements, depending on who you think is sending and who is receiving. Forget about them, they are confusing – the above three cases are all you need to know about in practice.

One difficulty that frequently arises with newer or portable computers is that some manufacturers have abandoned the traditional 25-way D-connector, largely on the grounds of bulk, cost and redundancy. Some important computer and peripheral companies favour connectors based on the DIN series (invented in Germany) while others use D-connectors with fewer pin-outs, usually 9. Sometimes to you will see that male (pins sticking out) and sometimes female (holes) 25-pin D-connectors are required – you'll need a gadget called a gender-changer to make them talk to each other. *There is no standardization.* Even if you see two physically similar connectors on two devices which appear to mate together, regard them with suspicion. In each case, you must determine the equivalents of:

characters leaving computer (pin 2)
characters arriving at computer (pin 3)
signal ground (pin 7)

You can usually set the speed of the port from the computer's operating system and/or from Basic. There is no standard way of doing this; you must check your handbook and manuals. Most RS232C ports can handle the following speeds:

75, 110, 300, 600, 1200, 2400, 4800, 9600

and sometimes 50 and 19200 bits/s as well.

These speeds are selectable in hardware by appropriate wiring of a chip called a baud-rate generator. Many modern computers let you select speed in hardware by means of a DIL switch. The higher speeds are used either for driving printers or for direct computer-to-computer or computer-to-peripheral connections. The normal maximum speed for transmitting along phone lines is 1200 bits/s, although 2400 bits/s is beginning to appear.

Depending on how your computer has been set up, you may be able to control the speed from the keyboard – a bit of firmware in the computer will accept micro-instructions to flip transistor switches controlling the wiring of the baud-rate generator. Alternatively, the speeds may be set in pure software, the micro deciding at what speed to feed information into the the serial port.

In most popular micro implementations the RS232C cannot support *split-speed* working, i.e. different speeds for receive and transmit. If you set the port up for 1200 bits/s, it has to be 1200 receive and transmit. This is a nuisance in Europe, where 75/1200 is in common use both for viewdata systems and for some on-line services. The usual way round this is to have special terminal emulator software, which requires the RS232C hardware to operate at 1200/1200 and then slows down (usually the micro's transmit path) to 75 bits/s in software by means of a timing loop. An alternative method relies on a special modem which accepts data from the computer at 1200/1200 and then performs the slowing-down to 75 bits/s in its own internal firmware.

Terminal Emulators
We all need a quest in life; sometimes I think mine is to search for the perfect software package to make micros talk to the outside world. As in all such quests, the goal is only occasionally approached but never reached, if only because the process of the quest causes one to redefine what one is looking for.

These items of software are sometimes called communications packages or asynchronous comms packages, and sometimes terminal emulators, on the grounds that the software can make the micro appear to be a variety of different computer terminals. Until very recently most on-line computer services assumed that they were being examined through 'dumb' terminals – simply a keyboard and a screen, with no attendant processing or storage power (except perhaps a printer). With the arrival of PCs all this is slowly changing, so that the remote computer has to do no more than provide relatively raw data and all the formatting and on-screen presentation is done by the user's own computer. Terminal emulator software is a sort of halfway house between 'dumb' terminals and PCs with considerable local processing power.

Given the habit of manufacturers of mainframe and minicomputers to make their products as incompatible to those of their competitors as possible (to maximize their profits), many slight variants on the 'dumb' computer terminal exist – hence the availability of terminal emulators to provide, in one software package, a way of mimicking all the popular types.

Basic software to get a computer to talk through its RS232C port, and to take in data sent to it, is relatively trivial, although some programming effort is required to take care of the condition when the receiving computer is being sent data at a faster rate than it can handle – the transmitting computer must be told to wait. However, what the hacker needs is software that will make his computer assume a number of different personalities upon command, will store data as it is collected and print it out.

Two philosophies of presenting such software to the user exist: first, one which gives the naive user a simple menu which says, in effect, 'press a key to connect to database' and then performs everything smoothly, without distracting menus. Such programs need an 'install' procedure, which requires some knowledge, but most 'ordinary' users never see this. Normally, this is a philosophy of software writing I very much admire.

However, as a hacker, you will want the precise opposite. The second approach to terminal emulator software allows you to reconfigure your computer as you go on – there is plenty of on-screen help in the form of menus allowing you to turn on and off local echo, set parity bits, show non-visible control codes, etc. In a typical hack you may have only vague information about the target computer and much of the 'fun' to be obtained from the sport of hacking is seeing how quickly you can work out what the remote computer wants to 'see' – and how to make your machine respond.

Given the number of popular computers on the market, and the number of terminal emulators for each one, it is difficult to make a series of specific recommendations. What follows therefore, is a list of the sort of facilities you should look for:

On-line help You must be able to change the software characteristics while on-line – no separate 'install' routine. You should be able to call up 'help' menus instantly, with simple commands, while holding on to the line.

Text buffer The received data should be capable of going into the computer's free memory automatically so that you can view it later off-line. The size of the buffer will depend on the amount of memory left after the computer has used up the space required for its operating system and the terminal software. If the terminal software includes special graphics as in Apple Visiterm or some of the ROM packs used with the BBC, the buffer space may be relatively small. The software should tell you how much buffer space you have used and how much you have left at any one time. A useful adjunct is an *auto-save* facility which, when the buffer becomes full, stops the stream of text from the host computer and automatically saves the buffer text to disk. A number of associated software commands should let you turn the buffer store on and off , let you clear the buffer store or, when off-line, view the buffer. You should also be able to print the buffer to a 'line' printer (dot-matrix or daisy wheel or thermal image). Some terminal emulators even include a simple line editor, so that you can delete or adjust the buffer before printing. (I use a terminal emulator which saves text files in a form which can be accessed by my wordprocessor and use that before printing out.)

Half/full duplex (echo on/off) Most remote services use an echoing protocol: this means that, when the user sends a character to the host computer the host immediately sends back the same character to the user's computer, by way of confirmation. What the user sees on his computer screen, therefore, has been generated, not locally by his direct action on the keyboard, but remotely by the host computer. (One effect of this is that there may sometimes be a perceptible delay between keystroke and display of a letter, particularly if you are using a packet-switched connection – if the telephone line is noisy, the display may appear corrupt.) This echoing protocol is known as full duplex, because both the user's computer and the host are in communication simultaneously.

However, use of full duplex/echo is not universal and all terminal emulators allow you to switch the facility on and off. If, for example, you are talking into a half-duplex system (i.e. no echo), your screen will appear totally blank. In these circumstances, it is best if your software reproduces on the screen your keystrokes. However, if you have your computer set for half-duplex and the host computer is actually operating in full duplex, each letter will appear *twice* — once from the keyboard and once, echoing from the host, ggiivviinngg tthhiiss ssoorrtt ooff eeffffeecctt.

Your terminal emulator needs to able to toggle between the two states.

Data format/parity setting In a typical asynchronous protocol each character is surrounded by bits to show when it starts, when it ends, and to signify whether a checksum performed on its binary equivalent comes out even or odd. The character itself is described, typically, in 7 bits and the other bits — start, stop and parity — bring the number up to 10 (see chapter 2). However, this is merely one, very common, form and many systems use subtle variants — the ideal terminal emulator software will let you try out these variants *while you are still on line*. Typical variants should include:

Word length	Parity	No.stop bits
7	even	2
7	odd	2
7	even	1
7	odd	1
8	none	2
8	none	1
8	even	1
8	odd	1

(NB. Although the ASCII character set is 7 bit, 8 bits are sometimes transmitted with a 'padding' bit; machine code instructions for 8-bit and 16-bit machines obviously need 8-bit transmissions.)

Show control characters This is a software switch to display characters not normally part of the text that is meant to be read but which nevertheless are sent by the host computer to carry out display functions, operate protocols, etc. With the switch on, you will see line feeds displayed as ↑ J, a backspace as ↑ H, etc. (See Appendix IV for the usual equivalents.)

Using this device properly you will be able, if you are unable to get the text stream to display properly on your screen, to work out what exactly is being sent from the host and modify your local software accordingly. Control-show is also useful for spotting 'funnies' in passwords and log-on procedures – a common trick is to include ↑H (backspace) in the middle of a log-on so that part of the full password is overwritten. For normal reading of text, you have control-show switched off, as it makes normal reading difficult.

Macros This is the US term, now rapidly being adopted in the UK, for the preformatting of a log-on procedure, passwords etc. Typical connecting procedures to US services like The Source, CompuServe, Dow Jones, etc., are relatively complicated compared with using a local hobbyist bulletin board or calling up Prestel. Typically, the user must first connect to a packet-switched service like Telenet or Tymnet (the US commercial equivalents of BT's PSS), specify an 'address' for the host required (a long string of letters and numbers) and then, when the desired service or 'host' is on line, enter password(s) to be fully admitted. The password itself may be in several parts.

The value of the macro is that you can type all this junk in once and then send off the entire stream any time you wish by means of a simple command. Most terminal emulators which have this feature allow you to preformat several such macros.

From the hacker's point of view, the best type of macro facility is one that can be itself addressed and altered in software. Supposing you have only part of a password: write a little routine which successively tries *all* the unknowns; you can then let the computer attempt penetration automatically. (You'll have to read the emulator's manual carefully to see if it has software-addressable macros: the only people who need them are hackers and, as we have often observed, very few out-and-out hacker products exist!)

Auto-dial Some modems contain programmable auto-diallers so that frequently called services can be dialled from a single keyboard command. Again, the advantage to the hacker is obvious – a partly known telephone number can be located by writing some simple software routine to test the variables.

However, not all auto-dial facilities are equally useful. Some included in US-originated communications software and terminal emulators are for specific 'smart' modems, of which more later. There is often no way of altering the software to work with other equipment. In general, each modem that contains an auto-dialler has its own way of requiring instructions to be sent to it. If an auto-dialling facility is important to you, check that your software is configurable to your choice of auto-dial modem. Another hazard is that certain auto-diallers only operate on the multifrequency tones method ('touch-tone') of dialling used in large parts of the United States and only very slowly being introduced in other countries. The system widely used in the UK is called 'pulse' dialling. Touch-tone dialling is much more rapid than pulse dialling, of course. Finally, on the subject of US-originated software, some packages will only accept phone numbers in the standard North American format of: three-digit area code, three-digit local code, four-digit subscriber code. In the UK and Europe the phone number formats vary quite considerably. Make sure that any auto-dial facility you use actually operates on your phone system.

Auto-answer If your modem can answer the telephone, it is useful to have software that takes advantage of it. Strictly speaking, hackers don't need such a facility, but with this feature you can, for example, use a computer in your office or at a friend's to call your own. Any auto-answer facility should enable you to set your own password, of course – hackers don't like being hacked! Terminal packages will only have fairly crude auto-answer facilities. If you want more, you must purchase a bulletin board.

Format screen Most professional on-line and time-share services assume an eighty-column screen. The 'format screen' option in terminal emulators may allow you to change the regular text display on your micro to show eighty characters across by means of a graphics 'fiddle'; alternatively, it may give you a more readable display of the stream from the host by forcing line feeds at convenient intervals, just before the stream reaches the right-hand margin of the micro's 'natural' screen width.

Related to this are settings to handle the presentation of the cursor and to determine cursor movement about the screen. Normally you won't need to use these facilities, but they may help you when on line to some oddball, nonstandard service. Certain specific 'dumb' terminals like the VT52, which has become something of a mainframe industry standard, use special sequences to move the cursor about the screen – useful when the operator is filling in standard forms of information. Other settings within this category may allow you to view characters on your screen which are not part of the normal character set. The early Apples, for example, lacked lower case, presenting everything in capitals (as does the ZX81), so various ingenious 'fixes' were needed to cope. Even quite advanced home computers may lack some of the full ASCII character set, such oddities as the tilde ~ or backslash \ or curly bracket { }, for example.

Reassign keyboard A related problem is that home micro keyboards may not be able to generate all the required characters the remote service wishes to see. The normal way to generate an ASCII character not available from the keyboard is from Basic, by using a 'PRINT CHR$(*n*)' type command. This may not be possible when on line to a remote computer, where everything is needed in immediate mode. Hence the requirement for a software facility to reassign any little-used key to send the desired 'missing' feature. Typical requirements are BREAK, ESC, RETURN (when part of a string as opposed to being the end of a command), etc. When reassigning a series of keys, you must make sure you don't interfere with the essential functioning of the terminal emulator. For example, if you designate the sequence ‹ctrl›S to mean 'send a DC1 character to the host', the chances are you will stop the host from sending anything to you, because ‹ctrl›S is a common command (sometimes called XOF) to call for a pause. Incidentally, you can end the pause by hitting ‹ctrl›Q. Appendix IV gives a list of the full ASCII implementation and the usual 'special' codes as they apply to computer-to-computer communications.

File protocols When computers are sending large files to each other, a further layer of protocol, beyond that defining individual letters, is necessary. For example, if your computer is automatically saving to disk at regular intervals as the buffer fills up, it is necessary to be able to tell the host to stop sending for a period until the save is complete. On older time-share services, where the typical terminal is a teletypewriter, the terminal is in constant danger of being unable mechanically to keep up with the host computer's output. For this reason, many host computers use one of two well-known protocols which require the regular exchange of special control characters for host and user to tell each other all is well. The two protocols are:

Stop/start The receiving computer can at any time send to the host a stop (‹ctrl›S) signal, followed by, when it is ready, a start (‹ctrl›Q).

EOB/ACK The sending computer divides its file into blocks (of any convenient length); after each block is sent an EOB (end of block) character is sent (see ASCII table, appendix IV). The user's computer must then respond with a ACK (acknowledge) character.

These protocols can be used individually, together or not at all. You may be able to to use the 'show control codes' option to check whether either of the protocols are in use. Alternatively, if you have hooked on to a service which, for no apparent reason, seems to stop in its tracks, you could try sending an ACK or start (‹ctrl›F or ‹ctrl›Q) and see if you can get things moving.

File transmission All terminal emulators assume you will want to send, as well as receive, text files. Thus, in addition to the protocol settings already mentioned, there may be extra ones for that purpose, e.g. the Xmodem protocol very popular on bulletin boards. Hackers, of course, usually don't want to place files *on* remote computers. An associated facility is the ability to send non-ASCII (usually machine-code) files. Don't buy packages with error-correction protocols specific to only one software producer. Kermit, the most widely implemented mainframe error-correction protocol, is available from user groups.

Specific terminal emulation Some software has preformatted sets of characteristics to mimic popular commercial 'dumb' terminals. For example, with a ROM costing under £60 fitted to a BBC micro, you can obtain almost all the features of DEC's VT100 terminal, which until recently was regarded as something of an industry-standard and costing just under £1000. Other popular terminals are the VT52 and some Tektronix models, the latter for graphics display. ANSI have produced a 'standard' specification which permits 'cursor addressing' — i.e. the terminal will print at specific locations on the screen without the transmitting computer having to send lots of line feeds and spaces. The cursor is located by a series of short commands beginning with an ‹esc› character.

Baudot characters The Baudot code, or International Telegraphic Code No. 2, is the 5-bit code used in telex and telegraphy — and in many wire-based news services. A few terminal emulators include it as an option and it is useful if you are attempting to hack such services. Most software intended for use on radio link-ups (see chapter 9) operates primarily in Baudot, with ASCII as an option.

Viewdata emulation This gives you the full, or almost full, graphics and text characters of UK-standard viewdata. Viewdata TV sets and adapters use a special character-generator chip and a few, mostly British-manufactured, micros use that chip also — the Acorn Atom was one example. The BBC has a teletext mode which adopts the same display. But for most micros, viewdata emulation is a matter of using high-res graphics to mimic the qualities of the real thing, or to strip out most of the graphics. Viewdata works on a screen 40 characters by 24 rows and, as some popular home micros have 'native' displays smaller than that, some considerable fiddling is necessary to get them to handle viewdata at all. On the IBM PC, for example, you can normally only get an approximation of the graphics characters or fewer colours than the seven viewdata actually uses. To get the full effect you either need a special graphics board or a special replacement chip for the normal board — which then prevents you from getting the full graphics display of normal IBM PC programs.

In some emulators the option is referred to as Prestel or Micronet — they are all the same thing. Micronet-type software usually has additional facilities for fetching down telesoftware programs (see chapter 8).

Viewdata emulators must attend not only to the graphics presentation, but also to split-speed operation; the usual speeds are 1200 receive from host, 75 transmit to host. USA users of such services may get then via a packet-switched network, in which case they will receive it either at 1200/1200 full duplex or at 300/300.

Integrated terminal emulators offering both 'ordinary' asynchronous emulation and viewdata emulation are rare — I have to use completely different and non-compatible bits of software on my own home set-up.

```
BPARFEDSGIEECL          G1a        C  Op   MMain Index
WZT,,,,,,,,,,,,,,,,,,,,,,,,,,,,,,,,,,,,,,    WJD1 FOCUS^W=\ UQ QJGYOU'RE IN FOCUS
  BNow you can find...Christmas feature,     Bsnooker latest,TV guide...all at on
TZ,,,,,,,,,,,,,,,,,,,,,,,,,,,,,,,,,,,,,,      20 AGRICULTURE
     21 BUSINESS
     22 EDUCATION
     23 HOME BANKING
     24 MICROCOMPUTING
     25 TELESHOPPING
     26 TRAVEL
TZ,,,,,,,,,,,,,,,,,,,,,,,,,,,,,,,,,,,,,,     5 MESSAGE. SERVICESBMailbox,Telex L)
  6 NEWS, WEATHER, LEISURE, SPORT
TTZ,,,,,,,,,,,,,,,,,,,,,,,,,,,,,,,,,,,,,     7 A-Z INDEXESBto information & IPs
  8 CUSTOMER GUIDEBAll about Prestel
  9 WHAT'S NEW        AJC17th DECEMBER
TZ ,,,,,,,,,,,,,,,,,,,,,,,,,,,,,,,,,,,,,
```

```
              P R E S T E L        1a         Op

              Main Index

                1 FOCUS            YOU'RE IN FOCUS

              Now you can find...Christmas feature,
              snooker latest,TV guide...all at once

                 20 AGRICULTURE
                 21 BUSINESS
                 22 EDUCATION
                 23 HOME BANKING
                 24 MICROCOMPUTING
                 25 TELESHOPPING
                 26 TRAVEL

                5 MESSAGE SERVICES Mailbox,Telex Link

                6 NEWS, WEATHER, LEISURE, SPORT

                7 A-Z INDEXES to information & IPs

                8 CUSTOMER GUIDE All about Prestel

                9 WHAT'S NEW        17th DECEMBER
```

Screen formatting. The first image is what Prestel looks like viewed on a dumb terminal with various colour and format attributes appearing as ASCII characters. The second is the same page viewed via a videotex emulator.

Modems

Every account of what a modem is and does begins with the classic explanation of the derivation of the term: let this be no exception. Modem is a contraction of modulator-demodulator.

A modem taking instructions from a computer (pin 2 on RS232C), converts the binary 0s and 1s into specific single tones, according to which 'standard' is being used. In RS232C/V.24, binary 0 (ON) appears as positive volts and binary 1 (OFF) appears as negative volts. The tones are then fed, either acoustically via the telephone mouthpiece into the telephone line, or electrically by generating the electrical equivalent direct onto the line. This is the modulating process.

In the demodulating stage the equipment sits on the phone line listening for occurrences of preselected tones (again according to whichever 'standard' is in operation) and, when it hears one, it delivers a binary 0 or binary 1 in the form of positive or negative voltage pulses into pin 3 of the computer's serial port.

This explanation holds true for modems operating at up to 1200 bits/s; above this speed, the modem must be able to originate tones, and detect them according to *phase* as well, but since higher-speed working is unusual in dial-up ports – the hacker's special interest – we can leave this matter to one side.

The modem is a relatively simple bit of kit: on the transmit side it consists of a series of oscillators acting as tone generators and on receive it has a series of narrow band-pass filters. Designers of modems must ensure that unwanted tones do not leak into the telephone line (exchanges and amplifiers used by telephone companies are sometimes remotely controlled by the injection of specific tones) and also that, on the receive side, only the distinct tones used for communications are 'interpreted' into binary 0s or 1s. The other engineering requirements are that unwanted electrical currents do not wander down the telephone cable (to the possible risk of phone company employees) or back into the user's computer.

Until relatively recently the only UK source of low-speed modems was British Telecom. The situation is much easier now, but deregulation of 'telephone line attachments', which include modems, is still, as I write, so recent that the ordinary customer can easily become confused. Moreover, modems offering exactly the same service can vary in price by over 300 per cent. Strictly speaking, all modems connected to the phone line should be officially approved by BT or other appropriate regulatory authority.

At 300 bits/s you have the option of using direct-connect modems which are hard-wired into the telephone line, an easy enough, although illicit DIY exercise, or using an acoustic coupler in which you place the telephone handset. Acoustic couplers are inherently prone to interference from room noise but are useful for quick lash-ups and portable operation. Many acoustic couplers operate only in 'originate' mode, not in 'answer'. Newer commercial direct-connect modems are cheaper than acoustic couplers.

At higher speeds acoustic coupling is not recommended, although a 75/1200 acoustic coupler produced in association with the Prestel Micronet service is not too bad, and is now exchanged on the secondhand market very cheaply indeed.

I prefer modems that have proper status lights – power-on, line-seized, transmit and receive indicators. Hackers need to know what is going on more than most users.

British Telecom markets the UK services under the name of Datel (details are given in appendix V). The same appendix gives the type numbers of the BT modems that are often available on the secondhand market.

BT's system of connecting modems to the line are either to hard-wire the junction box (the two outer wires are the ones you usually need), a four-ring plug and associated socket (type 95A) for most modems, a five-ring plug and associated socket (type 96A) for Prestel applications – no, the fifth ring isn't used – and, for all new equipment, a modular jack called type 600. The USA also has a modular jack, but, of course, it is not compatible.

Modern modem design is greatly aided by a wonder chip called the AMD 7910. This contains nearly all the facilities to modulate and demodulate the tones associated with the popular speed services both in the CCITT and Bell standards. The only omission – not always made clear in the advertisements – is services using 1200/1200 full duplex, i.e. V.22 and Bell 212A.

Building a modem is now largely a question of adding a few peripheral components, some switches and indicator lights and a box. In deciding which 'world standard' modem to purchase, hackers should consider the following features:

1 Status lights – you need to be able to see what is happening on the line.

2 Auto-answer – this enables your computer to answer the phone automatically: the modem sends a signal to the computer, usually through pin 22 of the standard D25 connector. With auto-answer your own computer can become a 'host' so that others can call into it. You will need bulletin-board-type software for this.

3 Auto-dial – a pulse dialler and associated firmware are included in some more expensive models. You should ascertain whether the auto-dialler operates on the telephone system you intend to hook the modem up to – some of the US 'smart' modems present difficulties outside the States. You will of course need software in your micro to address the firmware in the modem – and the software has to be part of your terminal emulator, otherwise you gain nothing in convenience. However, with appropriate software, you can get your computer to try a whole bank of numbers one after the other (see p. 168).

4 D25 connector – this is the official 'approved' RS232C/V.24 physical connection – useful from the point of view of easy hook-up. A number of lower-cost models substitute alternative DIN connectors. You must be prepared to solder up your own cables to be sure of connecting up properly.

5 Documentation – I always prefer items to be accompanied by proper instructions. Since hackers tend to want to use equipment in unorthodox ways, they should look for good documentation too.

6 Hardware/software switching: cheaper versions merely give you a switch on the front enabling you to change speeds, originate or answer mode and CCITT or Bell tones. More expensive ones – called 'intelligent' or 'smart' modems – feature firmware which allows your computer to send specially formatted instructions to change speed, answer the phone, hang up, dial out under program control or store a list of frequently used phone numbers. Such modems can also often read and monitor the status of a telephone call, reporting back that a connection has been made, or that a number is busy, and so on.

The drawback is that you must have terminal emulator software capable of using all these functions. Until recently there has been no standard instruction set. You can even find the situation where software and modem firmware conflict – for example, one viewdata emulator package I rather like uses ‹esc› as a prefix to most of its major commands. And ‹esc› is also used as a prefix for an intelligent modem I had for a while. However, a standard based on those devised in the States by the D.C. Hayes company is now emerging. The Hayes modem protocols have become rather like the Epson codes for dot-matrix printers. All Hayes commands to the modem begin with the prefix AT. You can find the common AT commands in appendix V.

Finally, a word on build-your-own modems. A number of popular electronics magazines and mail-order houses have offered modem designs. Such modems are not likely to be approved for direct connection to the public telephone network. However, most of them work. If you are uncertain of your kit-constructing skills, however, remember badly built modems can be dangerous both to your computer and to the telephone network.

Test Equipment

Various items of useful test equipment occasionally appear on the secondhand market, via mail order, in computer junk shops, in the flea-market section of exhibitions and via computer clubs. It is worth searching out a cable 'break-out' box. This lets you restrap a RS232C cable without getting a soldering iron – the various lines are brought out onto an accessible matrix and you use small connectors to make (or break) the links you require. It is useful if you have an 'unknown' modem, or an unusually configured computer.

Related, but much more expensive, is a RS232C/V.24 analyser – this gives LED status lights for each of the important lines, so you can see what is happening.

Lastly, if you are a very rich and enthusiastic hacker, you can buy a protocol analyser. This is usually a portable device with a VDU, full keyboard and some very clever firmware which examines the telephone line or RS232C port and carries out tests to see which of several popular data-comms protocols is in use. Hewlett Packard do a nice range. Protocol analysers will handle synchronous transmissions as well as asynchronous. Cost: £1500 and up ... and up ... and up.

4 Targets

Wherever hackers gather, talk soon moves from past achievements and adventures to speculation about what new territory might be explored. It says much about the compartmentalization of computer specialities in general and the isolation of micro owners from mainstream activities in particular that a great deal of this discussion is like that of navigators in the days before Columbus; the charts are unreliable, full of blank spaces and confounded with myth.

In this chapter I am attempting to provide a series of notes on the main types of services potentially available on dial-up and give some idea of the sorts of protocols and conventions employed. The idea is to give voyagers an outline atlas of what is interesting and possible – and what is not.

On-Line Hosts

On-line services were the first form of electronic publishing; a series of big storage computers – and, on occasion, associated dedicated networks – act as hosts to a group of individual databases by providing not only mass data storage and the appropriate 'search language' to access it, but also the means for registering, logging and billing users. Typically users access the on-line hosts via a phone number which links into a public data network using packet switching; there is more on these networks in chapter 7.

The on-line business began relatively by accident; large corporations and institutions involved in complicated technological developments found that their libraries simply couldn't keep track of the publication of relevant new scientific papers and decided to maintain indexes of the papers by name, author, subject matter, and so on, on computer. One of the first of these was the armaments and aircraft company, Lockheed Corporation.

In time the scope of these indices expanded and developed and outsiders – subcontractors, research agencies, universities, government employees, etc., were granted access. Other organizations with similar information-handling requirements asked if space could be found on the computer for their needs.

Eventually Lockheed – and others – recognized the beginnings of a quite separate business; in Lockheed's case it lead to the foundation of Dialog, which today acts as host and marketing agent for over 300 separate databases. A cut-down version of Dialog, marketed under the name Knowledge Index, is available at tariff levels affordable by the private user. It currently contains about thirty databases and is accessable outside normal office hours. Other on-line hosts include BRS (Bibliographic Retrieval Services), Comshare (used for sophisticated financial modelling), DataStar, Blaise (British Library), I.P. Sharp, and Euronet-Diane.

On-line services, particularly the older ones, are not especially user-friendly by modern standards. They were set up at a time when both core and storage memory were expensive and the search languages tend to abbreviated and formal. Typically, they are used, not by the eventual customer for the information, but by professional intermediaries – librarians and the like – who have undertaken special courses. Originally on-line hosts were accessed by dumb terminals, usually teletypewriters like the Texas Whisperwriter portable with built-in acoustic modem, rather than VDUs.

The Dialog search language is fairly typical: the host sends a '?' prompt. You start a search with the word 'begin' followed by a four-letter abbreviation of the section you wish to use – COMP for computers, EDUC for education, MAGA for magazines, and so on. Each section is broken down into individual databases and you must then select which one you wish to search. The command word for searching by keyword is 'find'. Dialog comes back with the number of 'hits' corresponding to your request and, when you feel you have narrowed down the search sufficiently, you can ask it to 'display' in long, medium or short formats.

Here is a typical search – the commands are abbreviated: 'b' for 'begin', 'f' for 'find', and so on.

```
?b MAGA

Now in MAGAZINES (MAGA) Section
  Magazine Index (MAGA1) Database
(Copyright 1984 Information Access Corp)

?f comput? and fraud
PROCESSING
              25274   COMPUT?
               1138   FRAUD
         S1     23    COMPUT? AND FRAUD

?d s1/L/1-23
1/L/1
1920876
   Fail-safe credit cards    (computer chips embedded in card will
prevent counterfeiting and illegal use)
   Slomski, Anita
   Consumers Digest    v24 p16(1)   May-June   1985
   CODEN: CNDGA
```

```
SIC CODE: 6153
DESCRIPTORS:  credit card security measures; semiconductor
chips usage; counterfeits and counterfeiting prevention; credit
card fraud prevention; smart cards technological innovations


1/L/2
etc
```

The 'comput?' request includes a wild card to cover computer, computers, computing and other variants. The 'S1' is the way Dialog identifies my own first search – I can refine it later. 'D s1/L/1-23' is the command to tell Dialog to display the results of my search 1 in long format and to include items 1 through 23 (in fact, the lot).

Dialog has the usual Boolean operators – and, not, etc. but lacks some of the features found on more recently set-up systems. It won't let you work by date ranges and it won't let you specify that if two keywords are selected they must occur within a given number of words of each other. However, master Dialog and most other information-retrieval search languages will become obvious.

Today the trend is to use 'front-end' intelligent software on an IBM PC which allows the naive user to pose his/her questions informally while off line; the software then redefines the information request into the formal language of the on-line host (the user does not witness this process) and then goes on line via an auto-dial modem to extract the information as swiftly and efficiently as possible.

On-line services require the use of a whole series of passwords – the usual NUI and NUA for PSS (see chapter 7); another to reach the host; yet another for the specific information service required. Charges are either for connect time or per record retrieved, or sometimes a combination.

There are two broad categories of on-line service: *Bibliographic*, which merely indexes the *existence* of an article or book – you must then find a physical copy to read – Dialog is an example of this, though you can, at some expense, order hard copy via the system; and *Source*, which contains the article (or extract thereof) itself. *Full-text* services not only contain the complete article or book but will, if required, search the entire text (as opposed to mere keywords) to locate the desired information. An example of this is LEXIS, a vast legal database which contains nearly all important US and English law judgments as well as statutes.

News Services
The vast majority of news services, even today, are not, in the strictest sense, computer-based, although computers play an important role in assembling the information and, depending on the nature of the newspaper or radio or TV station receiving it, its subsequent handling.

The world's big press agencies – United Press, Associated Press, Reuters, Agence France Presse, Tass, Xinhua, PAP, VoA – use telex techniques to broadcast their stories. Permanent leased telegraphy lines exist between agencies and customers and the technology is pure telex: the 5-bit Baudot code (rather than ASCII) is adopted, giving capital letters only, and 'mark' and 'space' are sent by changing voltage conditions on the line rather than by different audio tones. Speeds are 50 or 75 bits/s.

The user cannot interrogate the agency in any way. The stories come in a single stream which is collected on rolls of paper and then used as per the contract between agency and subscriber.

To hack a news-agency line you will need to get physically near the appropriate leased line, tap in by means of an inductive loop, and convert the changing voltage levels (± 80 volts on the line) into something your RS232C port can handle. You will then need software to translate the Baudot code into the ASCII which your computer can handle internally and display on screen or print to a file. The Baudot code is given in appendix IV.

None of this is easy and will probably involve breaches of several laws, including theft of copyright material! However a number of news agencies also transmit services by radio, in which case the signals can be hijacked with a short-wave receiver. Chapter 9 explains.

Recent news digests are available in videotex format from the Press Association News File service.

As the world's great newspapers increasingly move to electronic means of production – journalists working at VDUs, subeditors assembling pages and direct input into phototypesetters – the additional cost to each newspaper of creating its own morgue is relatively slight and we can expect to see many more commercial services, provided there is not too much opposition from print unions.

In the meantime other publishing organizations have sought to make articles – extracts or complete – from leading magazines available also. Two UK examples are Finsbury Data Services' Textline and Datasolve's World Reporter, the latter including material from the BBC's monitoring service, the *Washington Post*, Associated Press, the *Economist* and the *Guardian*. Textline is an abstract service, but World Reporter gives the full text. In October 1984 it already held 500 million English words. In the USA there is NEXIS, which shares resources with LEXIS. NEXIS held 16 million full-text articles at that same date. A slightly less expensive service available is called Newsnet, but all these services are costly for casual use. They are accessed by dial-up using ordinary asynchronous protocols.

The London *Times* has launched an ambitious venture to provide educational services for schools under the name *The Times* Network. Many electronic newsrooms also have dial-in ports for reporters out on the job; depending on the system, these ports not only allow the reporter to transmit his or her story from a portable computer, but may also, like Basys Newsfury used by Channel 4 News, let them see news agency tapes, read headlines and send electronic mail. Such systems have been the subject of considerable hacker speculation.

Financial Services

The financial world can afford more computer aids than any other nongovernmental sector. The vast potential profits that can be made by trading huge blocks of currency, securities or commodities – and the extraordinary advantages that a slight 'edge' in information can bring – have meant that the City, Wall Street and the equivalents in Hong Kong, Japan and major European capitals have been in the forefront of getting the most from high-speed comms.

Ten years ago the sole form of instant financial information was the tickertape – telegraphy technology delivering the latest share price movements in a highly abbreviated form. As with its news equivalents, these were (and are, for the services still exist) broadcast services sent along leased telegraph lines. The user could only watch, and 'interrogation' consisted of backtracking along a tape of paper.

Extel (Exchange Telegraph) continues to use this technique for some of its services, like FNS, although it is gradually upgrading by using viewdata and intelligent terminals for the Examiner service. It also runs a dial-up Stock Exchange prices service called PriceLine; once you are logged in, the command ACT will list the most active shares of the moment.

However, it was Reuters just over ten years ago that put together the first packages which gave some intelligence and 'questioning power' to the end user. Each Reuters Monitor is intelligent, containing (usually) a DEC PDP 8 series mini and some firmware which accepts and selects the stream of data from the host at the far end of the leased line, marshals interrogation requests and takes care of the local display. Information is formatted in 'pages' rather like viewdata frames, but without the colour. There is little point in eavesdropping into a Reuters line unless you know what the terminal firmware does. Reuters now face an aggressive rival in Telerate and the fight is on to deliver not only fast comprehensive prices services but international screen-based dealing as well. The growth of Reuters and its rivals is an illustration of technology creating markets – especially in international currency – where none existed before.

The first sophisticated Stock Exchange prices 'screens' used modified closed-circuit television technology. London had a system called Market Price Display Service – MPDS – which consisted of a number of TV displays of current prices services on different 'channels' which could be selected by the user. But London now uses TOPIC, a leased line variant on viewdata technology, although with its magazine-like arrangement and auto-screen refresh it has as much in common with teletext as Prestel. TOPIC carries about 2500 of the total 7500 shares traded in London, plus selected analytical material from brokers.

Datastream represents a much higher level of information and display sophistication – using its £40,000 plus p.a. terminals you can compare historic data – price movements, movements against sector indices, etc. – and chart the results.

The hacker's reward for getting into such systems is that you can see share and other prices on the move. None of these prices are confidential and could be obtained by ringing a stockbroker. However, this situation is likely to change as the City makes its move from the traditional broker/jobber method of dealing towards specialist market making – there will then be electronic prices services giving privileged information to specialist share dealers. TOPIC, for example, will upgraded to become SEAQ, and by the end of 1986 brokers will be able to trade through the system.

All these services are only available via leased lines – City professionals would not tolerate the delays and uncertainties of dial-up facilities. However, dial-up ports exist for demonstrations, exhibitions, engineering and as backup or for ad hoc access on IBM PCs – and a lot of hacking effort has gone into tracking them down.

In the United States, in addition to Reuters, Telerate and local equivalents of official streams of Stock Exchange and over-the-counter data, there is Dow Jones, best-known internationally for its market indices similar to those produced by the *Financial Times* in London. Dow Jones is in fact the owner of the *Wall Street Journal* and some influential business magazines. Its Dow Jones News/Retrieval service is aimed at businesses and private investors. It features current share prices, deliberately delayed by fifteen minutes, historic price data, which can be charted by the user's own computer (typically an Apple or IBM PC) and historic morgue-type company news and analysis. Extensions of the service enable customers to examine accounts of companies in which they are interested. The bulk of the information is US-based, but can be obtained worldwide via packet-switching networks. All you need are the passwords and special software.

Business Information

Business information is usually about the credit worthiness of companies, company annual reports, trading opportunities and market research. The biggest electronic credit data resource is owned by the international company Dun & Bradstreet; during 1985-86 it is due to spend £25 million on making its data available all over Europe, including the UK. The service, which covers more than 900,000 UK businesses, is called DunsPrint, and access is both on line and via a viewdata front-end processor. One of the features is to compare a company's speed of payment with that of norms in their industry sector. Another agency, part of Great Universal stores, CCN services, extensively used already by the big clearing banks, and with 3000 customers accessing information via viewdata sets, has recently also announced an extended electronic retrieval service of its own called Guardian Business Information. CCN's viewdata service is impressive – if you have a password you can check someone's credit rating (or your own) by giving *approximations* of name and address – the powerful software will select likely alternatives until you have found the person you want. Other UK credit services available electronically include UAPT InfoLink and Jordan Information services.

In addition, all UK companies quoted on the London stock Exchange and many others of any size which are not, have a report and analysis available from ICC (InterCompany Comparisons) which can be accessed via on-line dial-up (it's on Dialog), through a viewdata interface and also by Datastream customers. Dun & Bradstreet also have an on-line service called KBE covering 20,000 key British enterprises.

Prodigious quantities of credit and background data on US companies can be found on several of the major on-line hosts.

A valid phone number, passwords and extracts from the operations manual of one of the largest US services, TRW – it has credit histories on 90 million people – sat on some hackers' bulletin boards (of which much more later) for over twelve months during 1983 and 1984 before the company found out. No one knows how many times hackers accessed the service. According to the *Washington Post*, the password and manual had been obtained from a Sears Roebuck national chain store in Sacramento; some hackers claimed they were able to alter credit records, but TRW maintain that telephone access to their systems is designed for read-only operations alone, updating of files taking place solely on magnetic tape.

US market research and risk analysis comes from Frost & Sullivan. Risk analysis tells international businessmen which countries are politically or economically unstable – or likely to become so – and thus unsafe to do business with.

University Facilities
In complete contrast to computers that are used to store and present data are those where the value is to deliver processing power to the outside world. Paramount among these are those installed in universities and research institutes.

Although hackers frequently acquire phone numbers to enter such machines, what you can do once you are there varies enormously. There are usually tiers and banks of passwords, each allowing only limited access to the range of services. It takes considerable knowledge of the machine's operating system to break through from one to another and indeed, in some cases the operating system is so thoroughly embedded in the mainframe's hardware architecture that the substantial modifications necessary to permit a hacker to roam free can only be done from a few designated terminals or by having physical access to the machine. However, the hobbyist bulletin board system quite often provides passwords giving access to games and the ability to write and run programs in exotic languages – my own first hands-on experience of Unix came in exactly this way. There are bulletin boards on mainframes and even, in some cases, boards for hackers!

Given the nature of hacking, it is not surprising that some of the earliest japes occurred on computers owned by universities. Way back in the 1970s, MIT was the location of the famous 'Cookie Monster', inspired by a character in the then-popular 'Rowan & Martin Laugh-In' television show. As someone worked away at his terminal, the word 'Cookie' would appear across his screen, at first slowly wiping out the user's work. Unless the user moved quickly, things started to speed up and the machine would flash urgently: 'Cookie, cookie, give me a cookie.' The whole screen would pulse with this message until, after a while, the hacking program relented and the 'Monster' would clear the screen, leaving the message: 'I didn't want a cookie anyway.' It would then disappear into the computer until it snared another unsuspecting user. You could save yourself from the Monster by typing the word 'Cookie', to which it replied 'Thank you' and then vanished.

In another US case, this time in 1980, two kids in Chicago, calling themselves System Cruncher and Vladimir, entered the computer at DePaul University and caused a system crash which cost $22,000 to fix. They were prosecuted, given probation and were then made a movie offer.

In the UK many important university and research institution computers have been linked together on two special data networks called SERCNET and JANET. SERC is the Science and Engineering Research Council. Although most of the computers are individually accessible via PSS, SERCNET makes it possible to enter one computer and pass through to others. During early 1984 SERCNET was the target of much hacker attention; a fuller account appears in chapter 7 but, to anticipate a little, a local entry node was discovered via one of the London University college computers with a demonstration facility which, if asked nicely, disgorged an operating manual and list of 'addresses'. One of the minor joys of this list was an entry labelled 'Gateway to Universe', pure Hitchhiker material, concealing an extensive long-term multifunction communications project. Eventually some hackers based at a home counties university managed to discover ways of roaming free around the network.

JANET, the Joint University Network, operates in a similar way but is not confined in its subject matter to science and engineering. The expert hackers on JANET tend to be located, as you might expect, in university computer departments.

Banking

Prominent among public fantasies about hackers is the one in which banks are entered electronically, accounts examined and in some money moved from one to another. The fantasies, bolstered by underresearched low-budget movies and TV features, arise from confusing the details of several actual happenings.

Most 'remote stealing' from banks or illicit obtaining of account details touch computers only incidentally and involve straightforward fraud, conning or bribery of bank employees. There is *no* authentic account of a UK clearing bank suffering from a large-scale computer fraud; it is not that such frauds haven't taken place, just that the banks, fearful of their credibility with their customers, go to extraordinary lengths to conceal the crimes. These big frauds are invariably committed by employees; from the point of view of the outside criminal, however, when you think about the effort involved, human methods are much more cost effective. For hackers, however, the very considerable effort that has been made to provide security makes the systems a great challenge in themselves.

In the United Kingdom the banking scene is dominated a handful of large companies with many branches. Cheque clearing and account maintenance are conducted under conditions of high security with considerable isolation of key elements; interbank transactions in the UK go through a scheme called CHAPS, Clearing House Automatic Payments System, which uses the X.25 packet switching protocols (see chapter 7). The network is based on Tandem machines; half of each machine is common to the network and half unique to the bank. The encryption standard used in the US Data Encryption Standard. Certain parts of the network, relating to the en- and decryption of messages, apparently auto-destruct if tampered with. The service started early in 1984. The international equivalent is SWIFT, Society for Worldwide Interbank Financial Transactions, also X.25-based, which handles over 650,000 messages a day (1985) and is increasing at 15 to 20 per cent a year. If you want someone's 'balance' (how much they have in their account), the easiest and most reliable way to obtain it is with a plausible call to the local branch. If you want some easy money, steal a cheque book and cheque card and practice signature imitation. Or, on a grander scale, follow the example of the £780,000 Krugerrand fraud in the City. Thieves intercepted a telephone call from a solicitor or bank manager to 'authenticate' forged drafts; the gold coins were then delivered to a bogus company.

In the United States, where federal law limits the size of an individual bank's operations, and in international banking, direct attacks on banks have been much easier because the technology adopted is much cruder and more use is made of public phone and telex lines. One of the favourite techniques has been to send fake authorizations for money transfers. This was the approach used against the Security National Pacific Bank by Stanley Rifkin and a Russian diamond dealer in Geneva. $10.2 million moved from bank to bank across the United States and beyond. Rifkin obtained code numbers used in the bilateral test keys. Here the trick is to spot weaknesses in the cryptographic systems used in such authorizations. The specifications for the systems themselves are openly published, and one computer security expert, Leslie Goldberg, quite recently was able to take apart one scheme – proposed but not actually implemented – and show that much of the 'key' which was supposed to give high-level cryptographic security was technically redundant and could be virtually ignored. A surprisingly full account of his 'perfect' fraud appears in a 1980 issue of the journal *Computer Fraud and Security Bulletin*.

There are, however, a few areas where banking is becoming vulnerable to the less mathematically literate hacker. A number of international banks are offering their big corporation customers special facilities so that their treasury departments (that ensure, among other things that any spare million dollars are not left doing nothing overnight but are earning short-term interest) can have direct access to their account details via a PC on dial-up. A *Financial Times* survey in October 1985 identified thirteen major banking groups offering such services, many of them using the Geisco or ADP networks. Again, telebanking is now available via Prestel and some of its overseas imitators. Although such services use several layers of passwords to validate transactions, if those passwords are misacquired, since no signatures are involved, the bank account becomes vulnerable.

Finally, the networks of ATMs ('hole in the wall' cash machines) is expanding greatly. Each network has its own characteristics and software facilities are being added all the time. Here in the UK, banks are not the only people with ATMs; some building societies have banded together to set up their own network. As mentioned earlier in this book, hackers have identified a number of bugs in earlier versions of the machines. None of them, incidentally, lead directly to fraud. These machines allowed cardholders to extract cash up to a finite limit each week (usually £100). The magnetic stripe contains the account number, validation details of the owner's PIN (personal identity number), usually four digits, and a record of how much cash has been drawn that week. The ATM was usually off line to the bank's main computer and only went on line in two circumstances – first, during business hours, to respond to a customer's 'balance request' and, second, outside regular hours, to take into local memory lists of invalid cards which should not be returned to the customer and to dump out chequebook and printed statement requests. Hackers have found ways of getting more than their cash limit each week. The ATMs belonging to one clearing bank could be 'cheated' in this way: you asked for your maximum amount and then, when the transaction was almost completed, the ATM asked you, 'Do you want another transaction, yes/no?' If you responded 'Yes' you could then ask for – and get – your credit limit again, and again, and again. The weakness in the system was that the magnetic stripe was not overwritten to show you had had a transaction until it was physically ejected from the machine. This bug has now been fixed. A related but more bizarre bug resided for a while on the ATMs used by that first bank's most obvious high street rivals. In that case you had to first exhaust your week's limit. You then asked for a further sum, say £75. The machine refused but asked if you wanted a further transaction. Then, if you slowly reduced the amounts you were asking for by £5 ... £70, £65, £60 ... and so on, down to £10, you could then tell the ATM to cancel the last £5 transaction, and the machine gave you the full £75. Some hackers firmly believe the bug was placed there by the original software writer. This bug, too, has now been fixed. Neither of these quirks resulted in hackers 'winning' money from the banks involved; the accounts were in every case properly debited. The only victory was to beat the system.

For the future, I note that the cost of magnetic stripe reader/writers which interface to PCs is dropping to very low levels. I await the first inevitable news reports.

Electronic Mail

Electronic mail services work by storing messages created by some users until they are retrieved by their intended recipients. The ingredients of a typical system are: registration/logging-on facilities, storage, search and retrieval, networking, timing and billing. Electronic mail is an easy add-on to most mainframe installations, but in recent years various organizations have sought to market services to individuals, companies and industries where electronic mail was the main purpose of the system, not an add-on.

The system software in widest use is that of ITT Dialcom; it's the one that runs Telecom Gold, but another successful package is that used in the UK and the USA by Easylink, which is supported by Cable & Wireless and Western Union.

In the Dialcom/Telecom Gold service the assumption is made that most users will want to concentrate on a relatively narrow range of correspondents. Accordingly, the way it is sold is as a series of systems, each run by a 'manager': someone within a company. The 'manager' is the only person who has direct contact with the electronic mail owner and he in turn is responsible for bringing individual users onto his 'system' – he can issue 'mailboxes' direct, determine tariff levels, put up general messages. In most other services, every user has a direct relationship with the electronic mail company.

The services vary according to their tariff structures and levels; and also the sort of additional facilities – some offer bi-directional interfaces to telex; some contain electronic magazines, a little like videotex. Electronic mail is sometimes added on to existing networks – Dialog has added a feature called Dialmail; Geisco, an international networking resource for larger companies offers data transportation, databases and electronic mail – it doesn't want small users, however.

The basic systems tend to be quite robust and hacking is mainly concentrated on second-guessing users' IDs. Many of the systems have now sought to increase security by insisting on passwords of a certain length – and by giving users only three or four attempts at logging on before closing down the line. But increasingly their customers are using PCs and special software to automate logging-in. The software packages, of course, have the IDs nicely prestored.

Government Computers

Among hackers themselves the richest source of fantasizing revolves around official computers like those used by the tax and national insurance authorities, the police, armed forces and intelligence agencies.

The Pentagon, in fact, was hacked in 1983 by a nineteen-year-old Los Angeles student, Ronald Austin. Because of the techniques he used a full account is given in the operating systems section of chapter 6. NASA, the space agency, has also acknowledged that its e-mail system has been breached and that messages and pictures of Kilroy were left as graffiti. This leaves only one outstanding mega-target, Platform, the global data network of fifty-two separate systems focused on the headquarters of the USA's electronic spooks, the National Security Agency at Fort Meade, Maryland. The network includes at least one Cray-1, the world's most powerful number cruncher, and facilities provided by GCHQ at Cheltenham.

Although I know UK phone phreaks who claim to have managed to appear on the internal exchanges used by Century House (MI6) and Curzon Street House (MI5) and have wandered along AUTOVON, the US secure military phone network, I am not aware of anyone bold or clever enough to have penetrated the UK's most secure computers. In general it is far easier to obtain the information held on these machines – and lesser ones like the DVLC (vehicle licensing) and PNC (Police National Computer) – by human means than by hacking – bribery, conning and blackmail being the most obvious.

Nevertheless, there is an interesting hacker's exercise to be found in demonstrating how far it is possible to produce details from open sources of these systems, even when the details are supposed to be secret. But this relates to one of the hacker's own secret weapons – thorough research, the subject of the next chapter.

5 Hackers' Intelligence

The feature of hacking that most mystifies outsiders is how the phone numbers that give access to the computer systems and the passwords that open the data files ever reach hackers. Of all the ways in which hacking is portrayed in films, books and TV, the most misleading is the image of the solitary genius bashing away at a keyboard trying to 'break in'.

Most actual unauthorized computer invasions are quite simple: you acquire, from someone else – we'll see how in a minute – a phone number and a password to a system; you dial up, wait for the whistle, tap out the password, browse around for a few minutes and log off. You've had some fun, perhaps, but you haven't really done anything except follow a well-marked path. This isn't hacking in any worthwhile sense. After the first edition of this book was published I received rather too many letters from would-be enthusiasts asking me to please, please send them some 'real' telephone numbers. There's as much point to this as writing to the groundsman at Wembley requesting if you can be allowed to put a soccer ball between the goalposts – the *point* of football is to score when eleven men and a referee are trying to stop you and the *point* of hacking is to find things out for yourself.

Successful hacking depends on good research. The materials of research are all around: as well as direct hacker-orientated material of the sort found on bulletin-board systems and heard in quiet corners during refreshment breaks at computer clubs, huge quantities of useful literature are published daily by the marketing departments of computer companies and given away to all comers; sheaves of stationery and lorryloads of internal documentation containing important clues are left around to be picked up. It is up to the hacker to recognize this treasure for what it is and to assemble it in a form in which it can be used.

Anyone who has ever done any intelligence work, not necessarily for a government, but for a company, or who has worked as an investigative journalist, will tell you that easily 90 per cent of the information you want is freely available and that the difficult part is recognizing and analysing it. Of the remaining 10 per cent, well over half can usually be inferred from the material you already have, because, given a desired objective, there are usually only a limited number of sensible solutions. You can go further – it is often possible to test your inferences and, having done that, develop yet further hypotheses.

So the dedicated hacker, far from spending all the time staring at a VDU and 'trying things' on the keyboard, is often to be found wandering around exhibitions, attending demonstrations, picking up literature, talking on the phone (voice-mode!) and scavenging in refuse bins.

But both for the beginner and for the dedicated hacker who wishes to consult with his colleagues, the bulletin-board movement has been the single greatest source of intelligence.

Bulletin Boards

Since 1980, when good software enabling solitary microcomputers to offer a welcome to all callers first became widely available, the bulletin-board movement has grown by leaps and bounds. If you haven't logged onto at least one already, now is the time to try. At the very least it will test out your computer, modem and software – and your skills in handling them. Current phone numbers together with system hours and comms protocol requirements are regularly published in computer mags; once you have got into one, you will usually find current details of most of the others.

Bulletin boards nearly always operate on micros; they are single-user systems, although in every other respect they can look like big mainframes; the first one I ever used was running on a Tandy TRS-80, a 1978-79 generation personal computer. In the UK you will find two big families of bulletin board. The older generation, and by far the more numerous and useful, look like professional on-line services and usually run at 300 bits/s, 8 databits, no parity. After a while you'll learn the particular software packages in use from their way of displaying prompts and the sorts of commands available – TBBS by eSoft runs on TRS-80s and the IBM PC, Fido is just on the IBM PC, and there are others, not often used, for CP/M machines and the old Apple. The younger generation are viewdata- or videotex-compatible – they are like Prestel and are accessed at 75/1200 bits/s, 7 databits, even parity, which means that those with Micronet packages can use them. Because they operate on a frame-by-frame basis they are less flexible than the 300-bits/s packages. A popular videotex bulletin board package is CommunItel.

Somewhere on most boards you will find a series of special interest group (SIG) sections and among these, often, will be a hackers' club. Entrance to each SIG will be at the discretion of the sysop, the bulletin-board owner. Since the bulletin board's software allows the Sysop to conceal from users the list of possible SIGs, it may not be immediately obvious whether a hackers' section exists on a particular board. Often the sysop will be anxious to form a view of a new entrant before admitting him or her to a 'sensitive' area. It has even be known for bulletin boards to carry *two* hacker sections: one, admission to which can be fairly easily obtained; and a second, the very existence of which is a tightly controlled secret, where mutually trusting initiates swap information.

The first-timer, reading through a hackers' bulletin board, will find that it seems to consist of a series of discursive conversations between friends. Occasionally, someone may write up a summary for more universal consumption. You will see questions being posed; if you feel you can contribute, do so, because the whole idea is that a bulletin board is an information exchange. It is considered crass to appear on a board and simply ask, 'Got any good numbers?'; if you do, you will not get any answers. Any questions you ask should be highly specific, show that you have already done some groundwork, and make clear that any results derived from the help you receive will be reported back to the board. Confidential notes to individuals, not for general consumption, can be sent using the E-mail option on the bulletin board, but, remember, *nothing* is hidden from the sysop.

A flavour of the type of material that can be seen on bulletin boards appears from this slightly doctored excerpt (I have removed some of the menu sequences in which the system asks what you want to do next and have deleted the identities of individuals):

```
Msg#: 3538 *MODEM-SPOT*
01/30/84 12:34:04 (Read 39 Times)
From: xxxxxx xxxxxxxx
To: ALL
Subj: BBC/MAPLIN MODEMS
RE THE CONNECTIONS ON THE BBC/MAPLIN MODEM SETUP, THE CTS PIN IS USEDTO
HANDSHAKE WITH THE RTS PIN E.G. ONE UNIT SENDS RTS (READY TO SEND) AND THE
SECOND UNIT REPLIES CTS (CLEAR TO SEND). USUALLY DONE BY TAKING PIN HIGH. IF
YOU STRAP IT HIGH I WOULD SUGGEST VIA A 4K7 RESISTOR TO THE VCC/+VE RAIL (5V)
IN THE EVENT OF A BUFFER OVERFLOW. THESE RTS/CTS PINS ARE TAKEN LOW AND THIS
STOPS THE DATA TRANSFER. ON A 25WAY D TYPE CONNECTOR TX DATA IS PIN 2
RX DATA IS PIN 3
RTS IS PIN 4
CTS IS PIN 5
GROUND IS PIN 7


ALL THE BEST -- ANY COMMTO xxxxxx xxxxxxxx.
(DATA COMMS ENGINEER)

Msg#: 3570 *MODEM-SPOT*
01/31/84 23:43:08 (Read 31 Times)
```

From: xxxx xxxxx
To: xxxxxxx xxxxxxxxx
Subj: REPLY TO MSG# 3538 (BBC/MAPLIN MODEMS)
ON THE BBC COMPUTER IT IS EASIER TO CONNECT THE RTS (READY TO SEND) PIN TO THE
CTS (CLEAR TO SEND) PIN. THIS OVERCOMES THE PROBLEM OF HAND SHAKING.
SINCE THE MAPLIN MODEM DOES NOT HAVE HAND SHAKING,I HAVE PUT MY RTS CTS JUMPER
INSIDE THE MODEM.MY CABLES ARE THEN STANDARD AND CAN BE USED WITH HANDSHAKERS.
REGARDS

Msg#: 3662 #HACKER'S CLUB#
02/04/84 23:37:11 (Read 41 Times)
From: xxx xxxxxxx
To: ALL
Subj: PUBLIC DATA NET
Does anyone gnow what the Public Data Net is? I appear to have access to it,&
I daren't ask what it is'
Also, can anyone tell me more about the Primenet systems... Again, I seem to
have the means,but no info. F'rinstance, I have a relative who logs on to
another Prime Both of our systems are on Primenet, is there any way we can
communicate?
More info to those who want it...

<N>ext msg, <R>eply, or <S>top?
Msg has replies, read now(Y/N)? y

Reply has been deleted

<N>ext msg, <R>eply, or <S>top?

Msg#: 3739 #HACKER'S CLUB#
02/06/84 22:39:06 (Read 15 Times)
From: xxx xxxxxxx
To: xxx xxxx
Subj: REPLY TO MSG# 3716 (PRIMENET COMMS)
Ahh, but what is the significance of the Address-does it mean a PSS number, or
some thing like that? Meanwhile,I'll get on-line (via voice-link on the phone')
to my cousin, and see what he has on it....

Msg#: 3766 #HACKER'S CLUB#
02/07/84 13:37:04 (Read 13 Times)
From: xxxxxx xxx
To: xxxxx xxxxxxxxx
Subj: REPLY TO MSG# 3701 (PUBLIC DATA NET)
Primenet is a loal area network. I know of one in Poole, And BTGold use one
between their systems too. It is only an internal network, I suggest using PSS
to communicate between diffferent primes.   Cheers.

N ext msg, <R>eply, or <S>top?

Msg#: 3799 #BBC#
02/07/84 22:09:05 (Read 4 Times)
From: xxxxx xxxxxxx
To: xxxxx xxxxxx
Subj: REPLY TO MSG# 3751 (RGB VIDEO)
The normal video output BNC can be made to produce colour video by making a
link near to the bnc socket on the pcb. details are in the advanced user guide
under the chapter on what the various links do. If you require more I will try
to help, as I have done this mod and it works fine

Msg#: 935 #EREWHON#
09/20/83 01:23:00 (Read 90 Times)
From: xxxxx xxxx
To: ALL
Subj: US PHONE FREAKING
USA Phone Freaking is done with a 2 out of 5 Code.   The tones must be with 30
Hz, and have less than 1 % Distortion.

Master Tone Frequency = 2600 Hz.
>1 = 700 & 900 Hz
>2 = 700 & 1100 Hz
>3 = 900 & 1100 Hz
>4 = 700 & 1300 Hz
>5 = 900 & 1300 Hz
>6 = 1100 & 1300 Hz
>7 = 700 & 1500 Hz
>8 = 900 & 1500 Hz

>9 ? 1100 & 1500 Hz
>0 = 1300 & 1500 Hz
>Start Key Signal = 1100 & 1700 Hz
>End Key Signal = 1300 & 1700 Hz
> Military Priority Keys 11=700 & 1700 ; 12=900 & 1700 - I don't reccomend
using these. (
The method of use will be explained in a separate note. DO NOT DISCLOSE WHERE
YOU GOT THESE FREQUENCIES TO ANYONE!

Msg#:   936 *EREWHON*
09/20/83 01:34:43 (Read 89 Times)
From: xxxxx xxxx
To: ALL
Subj: UK PHONE FREAKING

The UK system also uses a 2 out of 5 tone pattern.

The Master Frequency is 2280 Hz
>1 = 1380 & 1500 Hz
>2 = 1380 & 1620 Hz
>3 = 1500 & 1620 Hz
>4 = 1380 & 1740 Hz
>5 = 1500 & 1740 Hz
>6 = 1620 & 1740 Hz
>7 = 1380 & 1860 Hz
>8 = 1500 & 1860 Hz
>9 = 1620 & 1860 Hz
>0 = 1740 & 1860 Hz
>Start Key = 1740 & 1980 ; End Keying = 1860 & 1980 Hz
>Unused I think 11 = 1380 & 1980 ; 12 = 1500 & 1980 Hz

This is from the CCITT White Book Vol. 6 and is known as SSMF No. 3 to some
B.T. Personnel.

The 2280 Hz tone is being filtered out at many exchanges so you may need quite
a high level for it to work.

Msg#:   951 *EREWHON*
09/21/83 17:44:28 (Read 79 Times)
From: xxxxxxxxxx
To: PHONE FREAKS
Subj: NEED YOU ASK ?
In two other messages you will find the frequencies listed for the internal
phone system controls. This note is intended to explain how the system could be
operated. The central feature to realise is that (especially in the USA) the
routing information in a call is not in the Dialled Code. The normal sequence
of a call is that the Area Code is received while the Subscriber No. is stored
for a short period. The Local Exchange reads the area code and selects the best
route at that time for the call.   The call together with a new "INTERNAThe
call together with a new "INTERNAL" dialling code is then sent on to the next
exchange together with the subscriber number. This is repeated from area to
area and group to group.   The system this way provides many routes and corrects
itself for failures.

The Technique. Make a Long Distance call to a number which does not answer.
Send down the Master Tone. (2600 or 22080 Hz) This will clear the line back,
but leave you in the system. You may now send the "Start key Pulse" followed by
the Routing Code and the Subscriber No. Finish with the "End Keying Pulse". The
system sees you as being a distant exchange requesting a route for a call.

Meanwhile back at the home base. Your local exchange will be logging you in as
still ringing on the first call. There are further problems in this in both the
USA and the UK as the techniques are understood and disapproved of by those in
authority. You may need to have a fairly strong signal into the system to get
past filters present on the line. Warning newer exchanges may link these
filters to alarms. Try from a phone box or a Public Place and see what happens
or who comes.

Example:- To call from within USA to UK:-
> Ring Toll Free 800 Number
> Send 2600 Hz Key Pulse

53

> When line goes dead you are in trunk level
> Start Pulse 182 End Pulse = White Plains N.Y. Gateway continued in next
message

Msg#: 952 *EREWHON*
09/21/83 18:03:12 (Read 73 Times)
From: xxxxxxxxxx
To: PHONE FREAKS
Subj: HOW TO DO IT PT 2

> Start Pulse 044 = United Kingdom
> 1 = Londof (Note no leading 0 please)
> 730 1234 = Harrods Department Store.

Any info on internal address codes would be appreciated from any callers.

Msg#: 1028 *EREWHON*
09/25/83 23:02:35 (Read 94 Times)
From: xxxx xxxxxxxx
To: ALL
Subj: FREEFONE PART 1

The following info comes from a leaflet entitled 'FREEFONE':

"British Telecom's recent record profits and continuing appalling service have
prompted the circulation of this information. It comprises a method of making
telephone calls free of charge."
.pa
Circuit Diagram:

```
                         0----o-------     -------o----0
                         :    '                   '    :
                         :    '                   '    :
                     L   o--------     --------o       P
                     I   :    '                   '    H
                     N   '                        '    O
                     E   o--                ----o      N
                     :    '                   '        E
                     :    '                   '        :
                     I   :    '                   '    :
                     N   o-------      --------o       :
                         :                             :
                         :                             :
                         :                             :
                         0-----------------------------0
```

S1 =
C1 =
D1 =
D2 =
R1 =

continued...

Msg#: 1029 *EREWHON*
09/25/83 23:19:17 (Read 87 Times)
From: xxxx xxxxxxx
To: ALL
Subj: FREEFONE PART 2

Circuit Operation:

The circuit inhibits the charging for incoming calls only. When a phone is
answered, there is normally approx. 100mA DC loop current but only 8mA or so is
necessary to polarise the mic In the handset. Drawing only this small amount is
sufficient to fool BT's ancient 'Electric Meccano'.

It's extremely simple. When ringing, the polarity of the line reverses so D1
effectively answers the call when the handset is lifted. When the call is
established, the line polarity reverts and R1 limits the loop current while D2
is a LED to indicate the circuit is in operation. C1 ensures speECh is
unaffected. S1 returns the telephone to normal.

Local calls of unlimited length can be made free of charge. Long disTance calls
using this circuit are prone to automatic disconnection, this varies from area
to area but you will get at least 3 minutes before the line is closed down.
Further experimentation should bear fruit in this respect.

Sith the phone on the hook this circuit is completely undetectable. The swItch
should be cLosed if a call iS received from an operator, for example, or to
make an outgoing call. It has proved extremely useful, particularly for friends
phoning from payphones with jammed coin slots.

Please DO NOT tell ANYONE where yoU found this information

Msg#: 1194 *EREWHON*
10/07/83 04:50:34 (Read 81 Times)
From: xxxx xxxxxx
To: ALL
Subj: FREE TEST NUMBERS

Free Test Numbers
=================
Here are some no's that have been found to work:
Dial 174 <last 4 figs of your no>: this gives unobtainable then when you
replace handset the phone rings.
Dial 175 <last 4 figs of your no>: this gives 'start test...start test...',
then when you hang-up the phone rings. Pick it up and you either get dial tone
whiah indicates OK or you will get a recording i.e 'poor insulation B line'
telLing you what's wrong. If you get dial tone you can immediately dial 1305 to
do a further test which might say 'faulty dial pulses'.
Other numbers to try are 182, 184 or 185.
I have discovered my exchange (Pontybodkin) gives a test ring for 1267.
These numbers all depend on you local exchange so It pays to experiment, try
numbers starting with 1 aS thEse are all local functIons. Then when you
discover something of interest let me know on this SIG.

Msg#: 2241 *EREWHON*
12/04/83 20:48:49 (Read 65 Times)
From: SYSOP
To: SERIOUS FREAKS
Subj: USA INFO
There is a company (?) in the USA called Loopmaniacs Unlimited , PO Box 1197,
Port Townsend, WA, 98368, who publish a line of books on telephone hacking.
Some have circuits even.   Write to M. Hoy there.

One of their publcns is "Steal This Book" at $5.95 plus about $4 post. Its
worth stealing, but don't show it to the customs!

Msg#: 3266 *EREWHON*
01/22/84 06:25:01 (Read 53 Times)
From: xxx xxxxxxx
To: ALL
Subj: UNIVERSITY COMPUTERS
As already described getting onto the UCL PAD allows various calls. Via this
network you can access many many university/research ck]]~puters To get a full
list use CALL 40 then HELP, select GUIDE. Typing '32' at the VIEW prompt will
start listing the addresses. Most of these can be used at the pad by 'CALL
addr' where addr is the address. For passwords yotry DEMO, HELP etc. If you
find anything interesting report it here.
HINT: To aviod the PAD hanging up at the end of each call use the LOGON command
- use anything for name and pwd. This seems to do the tricl.
Another number: Tel: (0235) 834531. This is another data exchange. This one's a
bit harder to wake up. You must send a 'break level' to start. This can be done
using software but with a maplin just momentarily pull out the RS232 conn. Then
send RETURNs. To get a list od 'classes' you could use say Manchesters HELP:-
CALL 1020300, user:DEMO pwd:DEMO en when you're on HELP PACX.

Msg#: 3687 *HACKER'S CLUB*
02/05/84 14:41:43 (Read 416 Times)
From: xxxx xxxxxxx
To: ALL
Subj: HACKERS NUMBERS

The following are some of the numbers collected in the Hackers SIG:
****
Commodore BBS (Finland)   358 61 116223
****
Gateway test   01 600 1261
PRESTEST (1200/75)   01 583 9412
Some usaful PRESTEL nodes - 640..Res.D (Martlesham's experiments
in Dynamic Prestel, DRCS, CEPT standards, Picture Prestel), 601
(Mailbox,Telemessaging, Telex Link - and maybe Telecom Gold),
651 (Scratchpad -always changing). Occasionally parts of 650 (IP
News) are not properly CUGed off. 190 sometimes is interesting
as well.
****
These boards all specialise in lonely hearts services !
The boards with an asterisk all use BELL Tones
*Fairbanks, AK, 907-479-0315
*Burbank, CA,   213-840-8252
*Burbank, CA,   213-842-9452
*Clovis, CA,   209-298-1328
*Glendale, CA,   213-242-1882
*La Palma, CA   714-220-0239
*Hollywood, CA, 213-764-8000
*San Francisco CA 415-467-2588
*Santa Monica CA, 213-390-3239
*Sherman Oaks CA, 213-990-6830
*Tarzana , CA,   213-345-1047
*Crystal River, FL904-795-8850
*Atlanta, GA,   912-233-0863
*Hammond, IN,   219-845-4200
*Cleveland, OH, 216-932-9845
*Lynnefield, MA, 617-334-6369
*Omaha, NE,   402-571-8942
*Freehold, NJ,   201-462-0435
*New York, NY,   212-541-5975
*Cary, NC,   919-362-0676
*Newport News,VA 804-838-3973
*Vancouver, WA, 206-256-6624
Marseilles, France 33-91-91-0660
****
Both USA nos. prefix (0101)
a) Daily X-rated Joke Service 516-922-9463
b) Auto-Biographies of young ladies who normally work in
unpublishable magazines on 212-976-2727.
c)Dial a w**K: 0101,212,976,2626; 0101,212,976,2727;

 Msg#: 3688 *HACKER'S CLUB*
 02/05/84 14:44:51 (Read 393 Times)
 From: xxxx xxxxxxx
 To: ALL
 Sub: HACKERS NUMBERS CONT
Hertford PDP 11/70 Hackers BBS:
Call 0707-263577 with 110 baud selected.
type: SET SPEED 300<CR>
After hitting CR switch to 300 baud.
Then type: HELLO 124,4<CR>
!Password: HAE4<CR>
When logged on type: COMMAND HACKER<CR>
Use: BYE to log out.
****
EUCLID   388-2333
TYPE A COUPLE OF <CR> THEN PAD <CR>
ONCE LOGGED ON TO PAD TYPE CALL 40 <CR> TRY DEMO AS A USERID WHY NOT
TRY A FEW DIFFRER DIFFERENT CALLS THIS WILL LET U LOG ON TO A WHOLE
NETWORK SYSTEM ALL OVER EUROPE!
YOU CAN ALSO USE 01-278-4355.
****
Unknown 300 Baud   01-854 2411
01-854 2499
****
Honeywell:From London dial the 75, else 0753(SLOUGH)
75 74199 75 76930
Type: TSS
User id: DD1003
password: Unwnown (up to 10 chars long)
Type: EXPL GAMES LIST to list gamec

```
To run a game type: FRN GAMES/(NAME).E for a fortran game.
Replace FRN with BRN for BASIC games.
*********
Central London Poly        01 637 7732/3/4/5
*********
PSS (300)                  0753 6141
*********
Comshare (300)             01 351 2311
*********
'Money Box'                01 828 9090
*********
Imperial College           01 581 1366
01 581 1444
*********
These are most of the interesting numbers that have come up over the
last bit. If I have omitted any, please leave them in a message.

Cheers, xxxx.
```

Msg#: 5156 *HACKER'S CLUB*
04/15/84 08:01:11 (Read 221 Times)
From: xxxxx xxxxxx
To: ALL
Subj: FINANCIAL DATABASES
You can get into Datastream on dial-up at 300/300 on 251 6180 -
no I don't have any passwords....you can get into Inter Company
Comparisons (ICC) company database of 60,000 companies via their
1200/75 viewdata front-end processor on 253 8788. Type *#*# when
asked for your company code to see a demo...

Msg#: 5195 *HACKER'S CLUB*
04/17/84 02:28:10 (Read 229 Times)
From: xxxxxxxx xxxxxxx
To: ALL
Subj: PSS TELEX
THIS IS PROBOBLY OLD HAT BY NOW BUT IF YOU USE PSS THEN A92348****** WHERE
**=UK TELEX NO. USE CTRL/P CLR TO GET OUT AFTER MESSAGE. YOU WILL BE CHARGED
FOR USE I GESS.

Msg#: 7468 *EREWHON*
06/29/84 23:30:24 (Read 27 Times)
From: xxxxxx xxxxxx
To: PHREAKS
Subj: NEW(OLD..) INFO
TODAY I WAS LUCKY ENOUGH TO DISCOVER A PREVIOUSLY UNKNOWN CACHE OF THE AMERICAN
MAGAZINE KNOWN AS TAP. ALTHO THEYRE RATHER OUT OF DATE (1974-1981) OR SO THEY
ARE PRETTY FUNNY AND HAVE A FEW INTERESTING BITS OF INFORMATION, ESPECIALLY IF
U WANT TO SEE THE CIRCUIT DIAGRAMS OF UNTOLD AMOUNTS OF BLUE/RED/BLACK/???
BOXES THERE ARE EVEN A FEW SECTIONS ON THE UK (BUT AS I SAID ITS COMPLETELY
OUT OF DATE). IN THE FUTURE I WILL POST SOME OF THE GOOD STUFF FROM TAP ON
THIS BOARD (WHEN AND IF I CAN GET ON THIS BLOODY SYSTEM''). ALSO I MANAGED TO
FIND A HUGE BOOK PUBLISHED BY AT&T ON DISTANCE DIALING (DATED 1975). DUNNO, IF
ANYBODY'S INTERESTED THEN LEAVE A NOTE REQUESTING ANY INFO YOU'RE AFTER CHEERS
PS ANYBODY KNOW DEPRAVO THE RAT?? DOES HE STILL LIVE?

Msg#: 7852 *HACKER'S CLUB*
08/17/84 00:39:05 (Read 93 Times)
From: xxxx xxxxx
To: ALL USERS
Subj: NKABBS
NKABBS IS NOW ONLINE. FOR ATARI & OTHER MICRO USERS. OPERATING ON 300 BAUD VIA
RINGBACK SYSTEM. TIMES 2130HRS-2400HRS DAILY. TEL :0795 842324. SYSTEM UP AT
THESE TIMES ONLY UNTIL RESPONSE GROWS. ALL USERS ARE WELCOME TO LOGON.
EVENTUALLY WE WILL BE SERVING BBC,COMMDORE VIC 20/64 OWNERS.+NEWS ETC.

Msg#:8154 *EREWHON*
08/02/84 21:46:11 (Read 13 Times)
From: ANON
To: ALL
Subj: REPLY TO MSG# !1150 (PHREAK BOARDS)

```
[][][][][][][][][][][][][]
[] PHREAK BOARD NUMBERS []
[]     ACROSS THE U.S.   []
[][][][][][][][][][][][][]
```

IF YOU KNOW OF A BOARD THAT IS NOT LISTED HERE, PLEASE LET ME KNOW ABOUT IT.

JOLLY ROGER	713-468-0174	PIRATE'S BEACH	305-865-5432
PIRATE'S CHEST	617-981-1349	PIRATE'S COVE	516-698-4008
PIRATE'S DATA CENTER	213-341-3962	PIRATE'S WAREHOUSE	415-924-8338
PIRATE'S SPACE STATION	617-244-8244	PIRATE'S PORT	512-345-3752
PIRATE'S OUTHOUSE	301-299-3953	PIRATE'S NEWSTAND][	213-373-3318
PIRATE'S HANDLE][	314-434-6187	PIRATE'S GOLDMINE	617-447-7428
PIRATE'S DREAM	713-997-5067	PIRATE'S SHIP	312-445-3883
PIRATE'S TRADE	213-932-8294	PIRATE'S MOUNTAIN	217-472-4287
PIRATE'S TREK	914-634-1268	PIRATE'S TREK][	914-967-2917
PIRATE'S TREK III	914-835-3627	PIRATE'S TREK IV	714-932-1124
PIRATE-80	305-225-8059	PORT OR THIEVES	305-798-1051
SANCTUARY	201-891-9567	SECRET SERVICE	213-932-8294
SECRET SERVICE][	215-855-7913	SHERWOOD FOREST	212-896-6063
SKELETON ISLAND	804-285-0041	GALAXY ONE	215-224-0864
BOCA HARBOR	305-392-5924	R.A.G.T.I.M.E.	217-429-6310
PIRATES OF PUGET SOUND	206-783-9798	KINGDOM OF SEVEN	206-767-7773
THE INSANITARIUM	609-234-6106	THE STAR SYSTEM	516-698-7345
HAUNTED MANSION	516-367-8172	ALPHANET	203-227-2987
WASTELANDS	513-761-8250	HACKER HEAVEN	516-796-6454
PIRATE'S HARBOR	617-720-3600	PHANTOM ACCESS	814-868-1884
SKULL ISLAND	203-972-1685	THE CONNECTION	516-487-1774
THE TEMPLE	305-798-1615	THE TAVERN	516-623-9004
SIR LANCELOT'S CASTLE	914-381-2124	PIRATE'S HIDEAWAY	617-449-2808
PIRATE'S CITY	703-780-0610	PIRATE'S PILLAGE	317-743-5789
PIRATE'S GALLEY	213-796-6602	THE PARADISE ON-LINE	512-477-2672
THE PAWN SHOPPE	213-859-2735	MAD BOARD FROM MARS	213-470-5912
MISSION CONTROL	301-983-8293	NERVOUS SYSTEM	305-554-9332
BIG BLUE MONSTER	305-781-1683	DEVO	305-652-9422
THE I.C.'S SOCKET	213-541-5607	TORTURE CHAMBER	213-375-6137
THE MAGIC REALM	212-767-9046	HELL	914-835-4919
PIRATE'S BAY	415-775-2384	CRASHER BBS	415-461-8215
BEYOND BELIEF	213-377-6568	ALCATRAZ	301-881-0846
PIRATE'S TROVE	703-644-1665	THE TRADING POST	504-291-4970
CHEYANNE MOUNTAIN	303-753-1554	DEATH STAR	312-627-5138
ALAMO CITY	512-623-6123	THE CPU	313-547-7903
CROWS NEST	617-862-7037	TRADER'S INN	618-856-3321
PIRATE'S PUB][	617-891-5793	PIRATE'S PUB	617-894-7266
PIRATE'S I/O	201-543-6139	BLUEBEARDS GALLEY	213-842-0227
SOUNDCHASER	804-788-0774	MIDDLE EARTH	213-334-4323
SPLIT INFINITY	408-867-4455	EXIDY 2000	713-442-7644
CAPTAIN'S LOG	612-377-7747	SHERWOOD FOREST][	914-352-6543
THE SILMARILLION][	714-535-7527	WARLOCK'S CASTLE	618-345-6638
TWILIGHT PHONE	313-775-1649	TRON	312-675-1819
THE UNDERGROUND	707-996-2427	THE SAFEHOUSE	612-724-7066
THE INTERFACE	213-477-4605	THE GRAPE VINE	612-454-6209
THE DOC BOARD	713-471-4131	THE ARK	701-343-6426
SYSTEM SEVEN	415-232-7200	SPACE VOYAGE	713-530-5249
SHADOW WORLD	713-777-8608	OXGATE	804-898-7493
OUTER LIMITS	213-784-0204	MINES OF MORIA][	408-688-9629
METRO	313-855-6321	MERLIN'S TOWER	914-381-2374
MAGUS	703-471-0611	GREENTREE	919-282-4205
GHOST SHIP III - PENTAGON	312-627-5138	GHOST SHIP][- ARAGORNS	312-644-5165
GHOST SHIP - TARDIS	312-528-1611	GENERAL HOSPITAL	201-992-9893
DATA THIEVES	312-392-2403	DARK REALM	713-333-2309
DANGER ISLAND	409-846-2900	COSMIC VOYAGE	713-530-5249
CORRUPT COMPUTING	313-453-9183	CAMELOT	312-357-8075
THE ORACLE	305-475-9062	PIRATE'S GUILD	312-279-4399
PIRATE'S PLANET	901-756-0026	HKGES	305-676-5312
CAESER'S PALACE	305-253-9869	MINES OF MORIA	713-871-8577
CRASHER BBS	415-461-8215	A.S.C.I.I.	301-984-3772

If anybody is mad enough to actually dial up one (or more!) of these BBs plea
log everything so that others may benefit from your efforts. IE- WE only have
to register once, and we find out if this board suits our interest. Good luck
and have fun! Cheers.

Msg#: 8163 *HACKER'S CLUB*
08/30/84 18:55:27 (Read 78 Times)
From: xxxxxxxx xxxxxxxx

To: ALL
Subj: *******************************
NBBS East is a relatively new bulletin board running from 10pm to 1230am on
0692 630610. There are now special facilities for BBC users with colour,
graphics etc. If you call it then please try to leave some messages as more
messages mean more callers, which in turn means more messages Thanks a lot, Jon

Msg#: 8601 *HACKER'S CLUB*
09/17/84 10:52:43 (Read 57 Times)
From: xxxx xxxxxxxx
To: xxxx xxxxxxxx
Subj: REPLY TO MSG# 8563 (HONEYWELL)
The thing is I still (sort of) work for XXX so I don't think they would be
too pleased if I gave out numbers or anything else, and I would rather keepmy
job. Surely you don't mean MFI furniture ??

Msg#: 8683 *HACKER'S CLUB*
09/19/84 19:54:05 (Read 63 Times)
From: xxxxx xxxxxxxxxx
To: ALL
Subj: DATA NODE
To those who have difficulty finding interesting numbers, try the UCL Data Node
on 01-388 2333 (300 baud).When you get the Which Service? prompt, type PAD
and a couple of CRs. Then, when the PAD>
prompt appears type CALL X00X00X, where is any(number orrange of numbers.
Indeed, you can try several formats and numbers until you find something
interesting. The Merlin Corn computer is 9002003. And it's difficult to trace
you through a data exchange! If anyone finds any interesting numbers, let me
know on this board, or Pretzel mailbox 012495225.

Msg has replies, read now(Y/N)? Y

Msg#: 9457 *HACKER'S CLUB*
10/11/84 01:52:56 (Read 15 Times)
From: xxxxxx xxxxxxxxxx
To: xxxxx xxxxxxxxxx
Subj: REPLY TO MSG# 8683 (DATA NODE)
IF YOU WANT TO KNOW MORE ABOUT THIS xxxxx PHIN PHONE xxxx xxxxxx
ON 000 0000

Msg#: 8785 *HACKER'S CLUB*
09/21/84 20:28:59 (Read 40 Times)
From: xxxx xxxxS
To: ALL
Subj: NEW NUMBER
NEW COMPUTER ON LINE TRY RINGING 960 7868 SORRY THATS 01 (IN LONDON) IN FRONT.
GOOD LUCK!

Please note that none of these hints, rumours, phone numbers and passwords are likely to work by the time you are reading this. However, I was both amused and alarmed to discover that, three months after the first edition of this book appeared, some of the numbers *were* still operational. Here is the timetable I had worked to: material siphoned off bulletin board, August 1984; lightly edited prior to delivery to publisher, November 1984; publication, March 1985; some numbers still valid after all the publicity, May 1985! Can I also resolve one puzzle which earlier readers seem to have set for themselves? No UK bulletin board has so far carried a super-SIG called Erewhon or even Nowhere. In mid-1984 the true name of the SIG was Penzance and it included many of the best hackers around, some of them actually using their real names. I made the name alteration on the printout using my wordprocessor's 'global change' facility, so that readers got the flavour of the SIG but not its identity. Since then the SIG's real name has been changed several times.

In the case of the US credit agency TRW, described in the previous chapter, valid phone numbers and passwords appear to have sat openly on a number of bulletin boards for up to a year before the agency realized. The owner of one of these, MOG-UR in Los Angeles, one Tom Tcimpidis, had his equipment seized by police on the prodding of Pacific Telephone. The event caused a panic among sysops on both sides of the Atlantic and it was suggested that the sysop could be held responsible for *all* material on a board, whether he had placed it there or not – or even personally seen the material. Some sysops even considered using 'naughty word' search programs to alert them to the messages that might cause trouble. However, in the end the charge against Tcimpidis was dropped through lack of evidence.

Some university mainframes have hackers' boards hidden on them as well.

It is probably bad taste to mention it, but of course people try to hack bulletin boards. An early version of one of the most popular packages could be hacked simply by sending two semicolons (;;) – when you did that, the system allowed you to become the sysop, even though you were sitting at a different computer; you could access the user file, complete with all passwords, validate or devalidate whomever you liked, destroy mail, write general notices, create whole new areas, and even access the fundamental operating system by exiting to the DOS.

Research Sources

The computer industry has found it necessary to spend vast sums on marketing its products and, while some of that effort is devoted to 'image' and 'concept' type advertising – to making senior management comfortable with the idea of the XXX Corporation's hardware because it has 'heard' of it – much more is in the form of detailed product information.

This information surfaces in glossies, in conference papers and in magazine journalism. Most professional computer magazines are given away on subscription to 'qualified' readers; mostly the publisher wants to know whether the reader is in a position to influence a key buying decision – or is looking for a job.

I have never had any difficulty in being regarded as qualified – certainly no one ever called round to my address to check up the size of my mainframe installation or the number of employees. If in doubt you can always call yourself a consultant. Registration is usually a matter of filling in a post-paid card. My experience is that, once you are on a few subscription lists, more magazines, unasked for, tend to arrive every week or month, together with invitations to expensive conferences in far-off climes. Do not be put off by the notion that free magazines must be garbage – in the computer industry, as in the medical world, this is absolutely not the case. Essential regular reading for hackers are *Computing, Computer Weekly, Network, Software, Datalink, Communicate, Communications Management, Datamation, Mini-Micro Systems* and *Telecommunications*.

The articles and news items often contain information of use to hackers: who is installing what where; what sort of facilities are being offered; what new products are appearing and what features they have. Sometimes you will find surveys of subsets of the computer industry. Leafing through the magazine pile that has accumulated while this chapter was being written, I have marked for special attention a feature on Basys Newsfury, an electronic newsroom package used, among others, by ITN's Channel 4 News; several articles on new on-line hosts; an explanation of new enhanced Reuters services; a comparison of various private viewdata software packages and who is using them; some puffs for new valued added networks (VANs); several pieces on computer security; news of credit agencies selling on line and via viewdata; and a series on defence data networks.

In most magazines, however, this is not all: each advertisement is coded with a number which you have to ring round on a tear-out post-paid (again!) 'bingo card'; each one you mark will bring wads of useful information. Be careful, however, to give just enough information about yourself to ensure that postal packets arrive and not sufficient to give the 'I was just passing in the neighbourhood and thought I would call in to see if I could help' sales rep a 'lead' he thinks he can exploit.

Another excellent source of information is exhibitions: there are the ubiquitous 'product information' sheets, of course, but also the actual machines and software to look at and, maybe, play with; perhaps you can even get a full-scale demonstration and interject a few questions. The real bonus of exhibitions, of course, is that the security sense of salespersons, exhausted by performing on a stand for several days – and the almost compulsory off-hours entertainment of top clients or attempted seduction of the hired-in 'glamour' – is rather low. Passwords are often written down on paper and consulted in your full view – all you need is a quick eye and a reasonable memory.

At both exhibitions and conferences it is a good idea to be a freelance journalist. Most computer mags have relatively small fulltime staff and rely on freelancers, so you won't be thought odd. And you'll have your questions answered without anyone asking 'And how soon do you think you'll be making a decision?'

Sometimes the lack of security at exhibitions and demonstrations defies belief. When ICL launched its joint venture product with Sinclair, the One-Per-Desk communicating executive workstations, it embarked on a modest roadshow to give hands-on experience to prospective purchasers. The demonstration models had been preloaded with phone numbers... of senior ICL directors, of the ICL mainframe at its headquarters in Putney and various other remote services.

Now that specialist computer programmes are appearing on television, it is not unknown for telephone numbers and passwords to be broadcast to several million people at a time. During the first run of the BBC's pioneering computer literacy series, which went out rather late at night, I got into the habit of using my video recorder as a time-shift device and used to view the following morning. One day, watching a section on viewdata, particularly private viewdata, I was surprised to see the telephone number and password of the Herts County Council private system being displayed on a viewdata adapter. It took but a moment to rewind the tape, inch the freeze frame forward slowly and garner the numbers at my leisure. I abandoned the rest of the programme and rushed to my viewdata set – and marched straight into the Herts machine. Two or three days later someone had obviously had a quiet word with them and the password was no longer valid. In the same series BBC accountants became alarmed when the *New York Times* Information Bank rang to tell them that their usage seemed to have gone up dramatically. A few days before, the Information Bank had been the featured subject. A dummy account had been set up so that the presenter could show log-on procedures in what was thought to be complete security. However, when the programme came to be taped, the dummy account failed to work. Ever resourceful, a floor engineer got hold of the BBC's real account number and arranged for the presenter to feed it in, saving, as he hoped, the day. Neither the presenter nor the show's director realized what had happened until the *New York Times* rang.

Beyond these open sources of information are a few murkier ones. The most important aid in tackling a 'difficult' operating system or applications program is the proper documentation. These can be obtained in a variety of ways. Sometimes a salesman may let you look at a manual while you 'help' him find the bit of information he can't remember from his sales training. Perhaps an employee can provide a 'spare' or run you a photocopy. In some cases you may even find the manual stored electronically on the system; in which case, print it out. Another desirable document is an organization's internal phone book – it may give you the numbers for the computer ports but, failing that, you will be able to see the *range* of numbers in use and, if you are using an auto-dial modem coupled with a search-and-try program, you will be able to define the search parameters more carefully. A phone book will also reveal the names of computer managers and system engineers; perhaps they use fairly obvious passwords.

Such material can often be found in rubbish bins. Susan Headley, the Californian hacker mentioned in the Introduction who later turned state's evidence to avoid sharing a prosecution with her former boyfriend (and who tends to appear rather frequently in TV documentaries about hacking), speaks of the habit of her local phone company to throw away complete system documentation even if only the smallest update was issued. Headley would march to the company's gates with a plastic carrier bag of aluminium cans asking if she could scavenge for more 'for charity'. She and her team always had nearly up-to-date documentation. In the UK British Telecom is also quite careless about its internal paperwork. It never ceases to astonish me what organizations leave in refuse piles without first giving them a session with the paper-shredder.

I keep my cuttings carefully stored away in a secondhand filing cabinet; items that apply to more than one interest area are duplicated in the photocopier. You never know when you might need them.

Inference

But hackers' research doesn't rely simply on collecting vast quantities of paper against a possible use. If you decide to target on a particular computer or network, it is surprising what can be found out with just a little effort. Does the organization which owns the system publish any information about it, in a handbook, annual report or house magazine? When was the hardware and software installed? Did any of the professional weekly computer mags write it up? What do you know about the hardware, what sorts of operating systems would you expect to see, who supplied the software, do you know anyone with experience of similar systems, and so on? With experience, you should be able to identify certain well-known 'host' environments.

By way of illustration I will describe certain inferences it is reasonable to make about the principal installation used by Britain's security service, MI5. At the end you will draw two conclusions: first, that someone seriously interested in illicitly extracting information from the computer would find the traditional techniques of espionage – suborning of MI5 employees by bribery, blackmail or appeal to ideology – infinitely easier than pure hacking; second, remarkable detail can be accumulated about machines and systems, the very existence of which is supposed to be a secret – and by using purely open sources and reasonable guesswork.

The MI5 databanks and associated networks have long been the subject of interest to civil libertarians. Few people would deny absolutely the need for an internal security service of some sort, or deny that service the benefit of the latest technology. But, civil libertarians ask, who are the legitimate targets of MI5's activities? If they are 'subversives', how do you define them? By looking at the type of computer power MI5 and its associates possess, it possible to see if perhaps they are casting too wide a net for anyone's good. If, as has been suggested, the main installation can hold and access 20 million records, each containing 150 words, and Britain's total population, including children, is 56 million, then perhaps an awful lot of individuals are being marked as 'potential subversives'.

It was to test these ideas out that two journalists, not themselves out-and-out hackers, researched the evidence upon which hackers have later built. The two writers were Duncan Campbell of the *New Statesman* and Steve Connor, first of *Computing* and more recently on the *New Scientist*.

The inferences work this way: the only computer manufacturer likely to be entrusted to supply so sensitive a customer would be British and the single candidate would be ICL. You must therefore look at their product range and decide which items would be suitable for a really large, secure, real-time database management job. In the late 1970s the obvious path was the 2900 series, possibly doubled up and with substantive rapid-access disk stores of the type EDS200.

Checking through back issues of trade papers it is possible to see that just such a configuration, in fact a dual 2980 with a 2960 as back-up and 20 gigabytes of disk store, were ordered for classified database work by 'the Ministry of Defence'. ICL, on questioning by the journalists, confirmed that they had sold three such large systems, two abroad and one for a UK government department. Campbell and Connor were able to establish the site of the computer, in Mount Row, London W1 (it has been moved since to MI5's largest site at Curzon Street House), and, in later stories, gave more detail, this time obtained by a careful study of advertisements placed by two recruitment agencies over several years. The main computer, for example, has several minis attached to it and at least 200 terminals. The journalists later went on to investigate details of the networks – connections between national insurance, the Department of Health, the police and the vehicle driving license systems.

In fact, at a technical level, and still keeping to open sources, you can build up even more detailed speculations about the MI5 main computer. ICL's communication protocols, CO1, CO2, CO3, are published items – you can get terminal emulators to work on a PC, and both the company and its employees have published accounts of their approaches to database management systems, notably CAFS, which, incidentally, integrates software and hardware functions to an unusually high degree, giving speed but also a great deal of security at fundamental operating system level.

Researching MI5 is an extreme example of what is possible; there are few computer installations of which it is in the least difficult to assemble an almost complete picture.

6 Hackers' Techniques

The time has now come to sit at the keyboard, phone and modems at the ready, relevant research materials convenient to hand, and see what you can access. In keeping with the 'handbook' nature of this publication, I have put my most solid advice in the form of a trouble-shooting appendix (I), so this chapter talks around the techniques rather than spelling them out in great detail.

Hunting Instincts
Good hacking, like birdwatching and many other pursuits, depends ultimately on raising your intellectual knowledge almost to instinctive levels. The novice twitcher will, on being told 'There's a kingfisher!', roam all over the skies looking for the little bird and probably miss it. The experienced ornithologist will immediately look low over a patch of water, possibly a section shaded by trees, because kingfishers are known to gulp the sort of flies that hover over streams and ponds.

So a good deal of skilful hacking depends on knowing what to expect and how to react. The instinct takes time to grow, but the first stage in such development is the realization that you need to develop it in the first place.

Tricks with Phones
If you don't have a complete phone number for a target computer then you can get an auto-dialler and a little utility program to locate it for you. An examination of the phone numbers in the vicinity of the target machine should give you a *range* within which to search. The program then accesses the auto-dial mechanism of the modem and 'listens' for any whistles. The program should enable the phone line to be disconnected after two or three 'rings' as auto-answer modems have usually picked up by then.

Such programs and their associated hardware are a little more complicated than the popularized portrayals suggest: you must be have software to run sequences of calls through your auto-dialler, the hardware must tell you whether you have scored a 'hit' with a modem or merely dialled a human being, and, since the whole point of the exercise is that it works unattended, the process must generate a list of numbers to try. In fact, you must use one of the new-generation 'smart' modems which are able to read the line and send a report back up into the RS232C port of the computer. Users of such programs in the USA have considerable advantages over those in the UK. Many areas in the USA use touch-tone dialling whereas the public network in the UK still uses pulse. This means that each call takes much longer to originate, and so the list of numbers that can be tried in a session is considerably reduced.

Logging On
You dial up, hear a whistle ... and the VDU stays blank. What's gone wrong? Assuming your equipment is not at fault, the answer must lie either in wrong speed setting or wrong assumed protocol. Experienced hackers listen to a whistle from an unknown computer before throwing the data button on the modem or plunging the phone handset into the rubber cups in an acoustic coupler. Different tones indicate different speeds and the trained ear can easily detect the difference – appendix III gives the common variants.

Some modems, particularly those on mainframes but increasingly some on semiprofessional bulletin boards, can operate at more than one speed – the user sets it by sending the appropriate number of carriage returns. In a typical situation the mainframe answers at 110 bits/s (for teletypewriters) and two carriage returns take it up to 300 bits/s – the normal default for asynchronous working. Some modems can sense the speed differences by the originate tone from the remote computer.

Some hosts will not respond until they receive a character from the user ... try sending a space or carriage return.

If these obvious things don't work and you continue to get no response, try altering the protocol settings (see chapters 2 and 3). Straightforward asynchronous protocols with 7-bit ASCII, odd or even parity and surrounded by one stop and one start bit are the norm, but almost any variant is possible. A PAD on PSS (see chapter 7) needs a ‹cr›‹cr›A2‹cr› to wake it up and tell it to send data in the form acceptable to a dumb terminal.

Once you start getting a stream from the host, you must evaluate it to work out what to do next. Are all the lines overwriting each other and not scrolling down the screen? Get your terminal software to insert carriage returns. Are you getting a lot of corruption? Check your phone connections and your protocols. Are you getting some recognizable characters, but jumbled up with others? Perhaps the remote computer expects to be viewed on an intelligent terminal which can accept instructions for formatting and highlighting data – like a VT52 or VT100. You will have to use a terminal emulator. The more familiar you are with your terminal software (see chapter 3) at this point, the more rapidly you will get results.

Passwords
Everyone thinks they know how to invent plausible and acceptable passwords – here are the ones that seem to come up over and over again:

HELP TEST TESTER SYSTEM SYSTEM MANAGER SYSMAN SYSOP ENGINEER OPS OPERATIONS CENTRAL DEMO SECRET LOVE SEX (plus the usual euphemisms for sexual activity) DEMONSTRATION AID DISPLAY CALL TERMINAL EXTERNAL REMOTE CHECK NET NETWORK PHONE FRED

Are you puzzled by the special inclusion of FRED? Look at your computer keyboard sometime and see how easily the one-fingered typist can find those four letters!

If you know of individuals likely to have legitimate access to a system you should find out what you can about them to see if you can second-guess their choice of personal password. Own names or those of loved ones or initials are the top favourites. Sometimes there is some slight anagramming and other forms of obvious jumbling. If the password is numeric, the obvious things to try are birthdays, home phone numbers, vehicle numbers, bank account numbers (as displayed on cheques) and so on. Sometimes numeric passwords are even easier to guess: I have found myself system manager of a private viewdata system simply by offering it the password 1234567890 and other hackers have been astonished at the results obtained from 11111111, 22222222, etc., or 1010101, 2020202.

It is a good idea to see if you can work on the mentality and known preoccupations of the legitimate password holder: if he's keen on classic rock 'n' roll, you could try ELVIS; a gardener might choose CLEMATIS; Tolkien readers almost invariably select FRODO or BILBO; those who read Greek and Roman literature at ancient universities often assume that no one would ever guess a password like EURIPIDES; it is a definitive rule that radio amateurs never use anything other than their callsigns.

Military users like words like FEARLESS and VALIANT or TOPDOG; universities, large companies and public corporations whose various departments are known by acronyms (like the BBC) can find those initials reappearing as passwords.

Poorly set-up access control systems (that's what the professionals call them) make life easy for the hacker. Many hosts show you how many characters are required for a valid password. Worse still, you may find that all the passwords on a particular system fall into a pattern or set of patterns; for example, there may be always a four-character alpha string, followed by four numbers followed by a further three characters, which are always an indicator for a particular location or office. When the original Prestel passwords were issued, those for information providers, those who had paid for space on which to edit on the service, always began with the three numbers 790 ...; this has now been changed.

One less publicized trick is to track down the name of the top person in the organization and guess a computer identity for him or her; the hypothesis is that he/she was invited to try the computer when it was first opened and was given an 'easy' password which has neither been used since nor wiped from the user files. A related trick is to identify passwords associated with the hardware or software installer; usually the first job of a system manager on taking over a computer is to remove such IDs, but often they neglect to do so. Alternatively a service engineer may have a permanent ID so that, if the system falls over, it can be returned to full activity with the minimum delay.

Nowadays there is little difficulty in devising theoretically secure password systems and bolstering them by allowing each user only three false attempts before the disconnecting the line, as does Prestel, for example. The real problem lies in getting humans to follow the appropriate procedures. Most of us can only hold a limited quantity of character and number sequences reliably in our heads. Make a log-on sequence too complicated, and users will feel compelled to write little notes to themselves, even if expressly forbidden to do so. After a while the complicated process becomes counterproductive. I have a encrypting/decrypting software package for the IBM PC. It is undoubtedly many times more secure than the famous Enigma codes of the Second World War and after. The trouble is that that you need up to twenty-five different fourteen-digit numbers, all different, of your specification which you and your correspondent must share if successful recovery of the original text is to take place. Unfortunately the most convenient way to store these sequences is in a separate disk file (get one character wrong and decryption is impossible) and it is all too easy to save the key file either with the enciphered stream or with the software master, in both of which locations they are vulnerable.

Nowadays many ordinary users of remote computer services use terminal emulator software to store their passwords. It is all too easy for the hacker to make a quick copy of a 'proper' user's disk, take it away, and then examine the contents of the various log-on files – usually by going into an 'amend password' option. The way for the legitimate user to obtain protection, other than the obvious one of keeping such disks secure, is to have the terminal software itself password-protected, and all files encrypted until the correct password is input. But then that new password has to be committed to the owner's memory ....

Passwords can also be embedded in the firmware of a terminal. This has been the approach used in many Prestel viewdata sets when the user can, sometimes with the help of the Prestel computer, program his or her set into an EAROM (electrically alterable read-only memory). If, in the case of Prestel, the entire fourteen-digit sequence is permanently programmed in the set, that identity (and the user bill associated with it) is vulnerable to the first person who hits 'viewdata' button on the keypad. Most users only program in the first ten digits and key in the last four manually.

A skilful hacker can make a terminal disgorge its programmed ID by sticking a modem in answer mode on its back (reversing tones and, in the case of viewdata, speeds also) and sending the ASCII ENQ (‹ctrl›E) character, which will often cause the user's terminal to send its identity.

A more devious trick with a conventional terminal is to write a little program which overlays the usual sign-on sequence. The program captures the password as it is tapped out by the legitimate user and saves it to a file where the hacker can retrieve it later.

People reuse their passwords. The chances are that, if you obtain someone's password on one system, the same one will appear on any other system to which that individual also has access.

Programming Tricks

In most longish magazine articles about electronic crime, the writer includes a list of 'techniques' with names like Salami, Trap Door and Trojan Horse. Most of these are not directly applicable to pure hacking, but refer to activities carried out by programmers interested in fraud.

The Salami technique, for example, consists of extracting tiny sums of money from a large number of bank accounts and dumping the proceeds into an account owned by the fraudsman.

Typically there is an algorithm which monitors deposits which have as their last digit '8'; it then deducts '1' from that and the £1 or $1 is siphoned off.

The Trojan Horse is a more generalized technique which consists of hiding away a bit of unorthodox active code in a standard legitimate routine. The code could, for example, call a special larger routine under certain conditions and that routine could carry out a rapid fraud before wiping itself out and disappearing from the system for good.

The Trap Door is perhaps the only one of these techniques that pure hackers use. A typical case is when a hacker enters a system with a legitimate identity but is able to access and alter the user files. The hacker then creates a new identity, with extra privileges to roam over the system, and is thus able to enter it at any time as a 'super-user' or 'system manager'.

Hardware Tricks
For the hacker with some knowledge of computer hardware and general electronics, and who is prepared to mess about with circuit diagrams, a soldering iron and perhaps a voltmeter, logic probe or oscilloscope, still further possibilities open up.

One of the most useful bits of kit consists of a small, cheap radio receiver (MW/AM band), a microphone and a tape recorder. Radios in the vicinity of computers, modems and telephone lines can readily pick up the chirp chirp of digital communications without the need of carrying out a physical phone tap. Alternatively, an inductive loop with a small low-gain amplifier in the vicinity of a telephone or line will give you a recording you can analyse later at your leisure. By identifying the pairs of tones being used, you can separate the caller and the host. By feeding the recorded tones onto an oscilloscope display you can freeze 'bits', 'characters' and 'words'; you can strip off the start and stop bits and, with the aid of an ASCII-to-binary table, examine what is happening. With experience it is entirely possible to identify a wide range of protocols simply from the 'look' of an oscilloscope. A cruder technique is simply to tape-record down the line and then play back sign-on sequences. The limitation is that, even if you manage to log on, you may not know what to do afterwards. A simple tape recording of a line fed into the rubber ears of an acoustic coupler, itself linked to a micro running a terminal package, will nearly always result in a good display.

Listening on phone lines is, of course a technique also used by some sophisticated robbers. In 1982 the Lloyds Bank Holborn branch was raided. The alarm did not ring because the thieves had previously recorded the 'all clear' signal from the phone line and then, during the break-in, stuffed the recording up the line to the alarm monitoring apparatus.

Sometimes the hacker must devise ad hoc bits of hardware trickery in order to achieve his ends. Access has been obtained to a well-known financial prices service largely by stringing together a series of simple hardware skills. Here, in outline, is how it was done.

The service is available mostly on leased lines, as the normal vagaries of dial-up would be too unreliable for the City folk who are the principal customers. However, each terminal also has an associated dial-up facility, in case the leased line should go down. In addition, the same terminals can have access to Prestel. Thus the hacker thought that it should be possible to access the service with ordinary viewdata equipment instead of the special units supplied along with the annual subscription.

Obtaining the phone number was relatively easy: it was simply a matter of selecting manual dial-up from the appropriate menu and listening to the pulses as they went through the regular phone. The next step was to obtain a password; the owners of the terminal to which he had access did not know their ID – they had no need to because it was programmed into the terminal and sent automatically. The hacker could have put a micro 'back to front' across the line, as explained above, and sent a ENQ to see if an ID would be sent back. Instead he tried something less obvious.

The terminal was known to be programmable, provided one knew how and had the right type of keyboard. Engineers belonging to the service had been seen doing just that. How could the hacker acquire engineer status? He produced the following hypothesis: the keyboard used by the service's customers was a simple affair, lacking many of the obvious keys used by normal terminals. The terminal itself was manufactured by the same company that produced a range of editing terminals for viewdata operators and publishers. Perhaps, if one obtained a manual for the editing terminal, important clues might appear.

A suitable photocopy was obtained and, lo and behold, there were instructions for altering terminal IDs, setting auto-diallers and so on. Now to obtain a suitable keyboard. Perhaps a viewdata editing keyboard or a general-purpose ASCII keyboard with switchable baud rates?

So far no hardware difficulties. An examination of the back of the terminal revealed that the supplied keypads used rather unusual connectors, not the 270° 6-pin DIN which is the Prestel standard. The hacker looked in another of his old files and discovered some literature relating to viewdata terminals. Now he knew what sort of things to expect from the strange socket at the back of the special terminal; he pushed in an unterminated plug and proceeded to test the free leads with a voltmeter against what he expected; eight minutes and some cursing later he had it worked out; five minutes after that he had built himself a little patch cord between an ASCII keyboard, set initially to 75 bits/s and then to 1200 bits/s as the most likely speeds; one minute later he found the terminal was responding as he had hoped.

Now to see if there were similarities between the programming commands in the equipment for which he had a manual and the equipment he wished to hack. Indeed there were: on the screen before him was the menu and ID and phone data he had hoped to see. The final test was to move over to a conventional Prestel set, dial up the number for the financial service and send the ID ... the hack had been successful.

The hacker himself was remarkably uninterested in the financial world and, other than describing to me how he had worked his trick, has now gone in search of other targets.

The current enthusiasm among computer security experts trying to sell hi-tech goodies to the paranoid is Tempest. Tempest is the name given to a series of US standards prescribing limits for electromagnetic radiation from computer installations and peripherals. It is possible to 'read' the contents of a VDU screen up to 300 metres away by tuning a suitable TV and radio receiver to the video and synchronizing frequencies of the display tube. The VDU's image is, of course, constantly being refreshed so that it is not too difficult to re-create. You can conduct some experiments yourself to see how it is done. The video elements of a display radiate out harmonics at frequencies between 100 MHz and 600 MHz. Take an ordinary domestic television and tune away from any broadcast signal (TV receivers in the UK cover the frequency band 470 MHz to 800 MHz) – you will see a picture of 'snow'. Now, attach a portable desk-top aerial – say with four or five elements. Aim the antenna at your 'target' VDU (not another television set). You should see the quality of the 'snow' change – become brighter. The TV is picking up the video elements of the transmission. You can't resolve an image at this stage because the sync elements necessary to stabilize an image don't radiate out nearly as well. If you take an AM (medium wave) receiver and tune around 1570 to 1600 kHz you should hear a buzz which increases as you approach the VDU. The buzzing sound is a harmonic of the VDU's line sync. In a Tempest eavesdropping unit, the two radio detectors – TV and medium-wave radio – are linked, the pulses from the medium wave radio synchronising the video elements the TV picks up and thus giving a stable image on the TV screen, they could be placed on a video recorder for later examination. Similar technology is used by the detector vans which occasionally roam the streets to see if you have paid your television licence. It is also possible to 'bug' a CPU – you can try it for yourself with a small portable radio. The difficulty is interpreting in a useful way what you pick up. GCHQ at Cheltenham are believed to have solved the problem of bugging typewriters, incidentally – each letter as it is impacted onto a piece of paper makes a slightly different sound – build up a table of these sounds, get an audio tape of someone typing, or a line printer, and a relatively simple computer program (once you have cracked the sound recognition problem) will regenerate the output for you – a marvellous way of bypassing encryption devices as the printers you try to bug in this way are presumabaly those handling 'clear' text. The National Security Agency first started a program to certify equipment as meeting Tempest standards as long ago as 1977, but it is only since 1985 that most civilians have become aware of the problem. Amateur eavesdropping kit could be built for around £30, though tuning up for each 'target' VDU isn't that simple outside the laboratory. Tempest eavesdropping works, but like other technologies that security consultants produce to scare potential clients such as bouncing lasers off windows to translate the vibrations of glass panes into the sounds of conversations held inside rooms, a multiplicity of practical engineering difficulties limits its use in the real world. What is also questionable is how much useful information can be obtained in this fashion – the most the technique offers is an imperfect window, one screen at a time, on what a user is viewing – and you need to get awkwardly close to the target before you get results. Spooks will do far better by more conventional hacking methods.

Operating Systems
The majority of simple home micros operate only in two modes – in Basic or machine code. Nearly all computers of a size greater than this use operating systems, essentially housekeeping routines which tell the processor where to expect instructions from, how to identify and manipulate both active and stored memory, how to keep track of drives and serial ports (and joysticks and mice), how to accept data from a keyboard, locate it on a screen, dump results to screen or printer or disk drive, and so on. Familiar micro-based operating systems include CP/M, MS-DOS, CP/M-86 and so on. More advanced operating systems have more facilities – the

capacity to have several users all accessing the same data and programs without colliding with each other, enlarged standard utilities to make fast file creation, fast sorting and fast calculation much easier. Under simple operating systems the programmer has comparatively few tools to help him; maybe just the Basic language which itself contains no standard procedures – almost everything must be written from new each time. But most computer programs rely, in essence, on a small set of standard modules – forms to accept data to a program, files to keep the data in, calculations to transform that data, techniques to sort the data, forms to present the data to the user upon demand, the ability to present results in various graphics, and so on.

So programs written under more advanced operating systems tend to be comparatively briefer for the same end result than those with Basic acting not only as a language but also as the computer's housekeeper.

When you enter a mainframe computer as an ordinary customer, you will almost certainly be located in an applications program, perhaps with the capacity to call up a limited range of other applications programs while staying in the one which has logged you on as user and is watching your connect time and central processor usage.

One of the immediate aims of a serious hacker is to get out of this environment and see what other facilities might be located on the mainframe. For example, if access can be had to the user log it becomes possible for the hacker to create a whole new status for himself, as a system manager, engineer, whatever. The new status, together with a unique new password, can have all sorts of privileges not granted to ordinary users. The hacker, having acquired the new status, logs out in his original identity and then logs back with his new one.

There is no single way to break out of an applications program into the operating system environment; people who do so seldom manage it by chance; they tend to have had some experience of a similar mainframe. One of the corny ways is to issue a BREAK or ‹ctrl›C command and see what happens; but most applications programs concerned with logging users onto systems tend to filter out 'disturbing' commands of that sort. Sometimes it easier to go beyond the logging-in program into an another 'authorized' program and try to crash out of that. Computers tend to be at their most vulnerable when moving from one application to another – making a direct call on the operation system. The usual evidence for success is that the nature of the prompts will change.

Thus, on a well-known mini family OS, the usual user prompt is

COMMAND ?

or simply

\>

Once you have crashed out the prompt may change to a simple

.

or

*

or even

:

it all depends.

To establish where you are in the system, you should ask for a directory – DIR or its obvious variants often give results. Directories may be hierachical, as in MS-DOS version 2 and above, so that at the bottom level you simply get directories of other directories. Unix machines are very likely to exhibit this trait. And once you get a list of files and programs ... well, that's where the exploration really begins.

In 1982 two Los Angeles hackers, still in their teens, devised one of the most sensational hacks so far, running all over the Pentagon's ARPA data-exchange network. ARPAnet was and is the definitive packet-switched network – more about these in the next chapter. It has been running for twenty years, cost more than $500 million and links together over 300 computers across the United States and beyond. Reputedly it has 5000 legitimate customers, among them NORAD, North American Air Defense headquarters at Omaha, Nebraska. Ron Austin and Kevin Poulsen were determined to explore it.

Their weapons were an old TRS-80 and a VIC-20, nothing complicated, and their first attempts relied on password-guessing. The fourth try, UCB, the obvious initials of the University of California at Berkeley, got them in. The password in fact was little used by its legitimate owner and, in the end, it was to be their downfall.

Aspects of ARPAnet have been extensively written up in the textbooks simply because it has so many features which were first tried there and have since become 'standard' on all data networks. From the bookshop at UCLA the hackers purchased the manual for Unix, the multitasking, multi-user operating system devised by Bell Laboratories, the experimental arm of ATT, the USA's biggest telephone company. At the heart of Unix is a small kernel containing system primitives; Unix instructions are enclosed in a series of shells and very complicated procedures can be called in a small number of text lines simply by defining a few pipes linking shells. Unix also contains a large library of routines which are what you tend to find inside the shells. Directories of files are arranged in a tree-like fashion, with master or root directories leading to other directories, and so on.

Ron and Kevin needed to become system 'super-users' with extra privileges if they were to explore the system properly; 'UCB' was merely an ordinary user. Armed with their knowledge of Unix, they set out to find the files containing legitimate users' passwords and names. Associated with each password was a Unix shell which defined the level of privilege. Ron wrote a routine which captured the privilege shell associated with a known super-user at the point when that user signed on and then dumped it into the shell associated with a little-used identity they had decided to adopt for their own explorations. They became 'Jim Miller'; the original super-user lost his network status. Other IDs were added. Captured privilege shells were hidden away in a small computer called Shasta at Stanford, at the heart of California's Silicon Valley.

Ron and Kevin were now super-users. They dropped into SRI, Stanford Research Institute, one of the world's great centres of scientific research; into the Rand Corporation, known equally for its extensive futurological forecasting and its 'thinking about the unthinkable', the processes of escalation to nuclear war; into the National Research Laboratory in Washington; into two private research firms back in California and two defence contractors on the East Coast; and across the Atlantic to the Norwegian Telecommunications Agency which, among other things, is widely believed to have a special role in watching Soviet Baltic activity. And, of course, NORAD.

Their running about had not gone unnoticed; ARPAnet and its constituent computers keep logs of activity as one form of security (see below), and officials both at UCLA (where they were puzzled to see an upsurge in activity by 'UCB') and in one of the defence contractors sounded an alarm. The KGB were suspected, the FBI alerted.

One person asked to act as sleuth was Brian Reid, a professor of electrical engineering at Stanford. He and his associates set up a series of system trips inside a Unix shell to notify them when certain IDs entered an ARPAnet computer. His first results seemed to indicate that the source of the hacking was Purdue, Indiana, but the strange IDs seemed to enter ARPAnet from all over the place. Eventually his researches lead him to the Shasta computer and he had identified 'Miller' as the identity he had to nail. He closed off entry to Shasta from ARPAnet. 'Miller' reappeared; apparently via a gateway from another Stanford computer, Navajo.

Reid, who in his sleuthing role had extremely high privileges, sought to wipe 'Miller' out of Navajo. A few minutes after 'Miller' had vanished from his screen, he reappeared from yet another local computer, Diablo. The concentration of hacking effort in the Stanford area lead Reid to suppose that the origin of the trouble was local. The most effective way to catch the miscreant was by telephone trace. Accordingly, he prepared some tantalizing, apparently private, files.

This was the bait, designed to keep 'Miller' on line as long as possible while the FBI organized a telephone trace. 'Miller' duly appeared, the FBI went into action – and arrested an innocent businessman.

But back at UCLA, they were still puzzling about 'UCB'. In one of his earliest sessions Ron had answered a registration questionnaire with his own address, and things began to fall into place.

In one of his last computer 'chats' before arrest, Kevin, then only seventeen and only beginning to think that he and his friend might have someone on their trail, is supposed to have signed off: 'Got to go now, the FBI is knocking at my door.' A few hours later, that is exactly what happened. Ron Austin was eventually convicted on twelve felony counts and imprisoned; after a few months he was released to perform 600 hours of community service work.

Computer Security Methods
Hackers have to be aware of the hazards of being caught: there is now a new profession of computer security experts and they have had some success. The first thing such consultants do is to attempt to divide responsibility within a computer establishment as much as possible. Only operators are allowed physical access to the

installation, only programmers can use the operating system (and under some of these, such as VM, maybe only part of the operating system), only system managers are permitted to validate passwords, and only the various classes of users are given access to the appropriate applications programs.

Next, if the operating system permits (it usually does), all accesses are logged; surveillance programs carry out an audit, which gives a historic record and also, sometimes, perform monitoring, which is real-time surveillance.

In addition, separate programs may be in existence the sole purpose of which is threat monitoring: they test the system to see if anyone is trying repeatedly to log on without apparent success (say, by using a program to try out various likely passwords), they assess if any one port or terminal is getting more than usual usage, or if IDs other than a regular small list start using a particular terminal – as when a hacker obtains a legitimate ID but one that normally operates from only one terminal within close proximity to the main installation, whereas the hacker is calling from outside.

Increasingly, in newer mainframe installations, security is built into the operating system at hardware level. In older models this was not done, partly because the need was not perceived but also because each such 'unnecessary' hardware call tended to slow the whole machine down. (If a computer must encrypt and decrypt every process before it is executed, if activity journals must be constantly written to, regular calculations and data accesses take much longer). However, the world's largest manufacturers now seem to have found viable solutions for this problem.

7 Networks

Until ten years ago the telecommunications and computer industries were almost entirely separate. Shortly they will be almost completely fused. Most of today's hackers operate largely in ignorance of what goes on in the lines and switching centres between the computer they own and the computer they wish to access. Increasingly, dedicated hackers are having to acquire knowledge and experience of data networks, a task made more interesting, but not easier, by the fact that the world's leading telecommunications organizations are pushing through an unprecedented rate of innovation, both technical and commercial.

Apart from purely local, low-speed working, computer communications are now almost exclusively found on separate high-speed data networks – separate, that is, from the two traditional telecommunications systems – telegraphy and telephone. Telex lines operate typically at 50 or 75 bits/s with an upper limit of 110 bits/s. The highest efficient speed for telephone-line-based data is 2400 bits/s. All of these are pitifully slow compared with the internal speed of even the most sluggish computer.

When system designers first came to evaluate what sort of facilities and performance would be needed for data communications, it became obvious that relatively few lessons would be drawn from the solutions already worked out in voice communications.

Analog Networks

In voice-grade networks the challenge had been to squeeze as many *analog* signals down limited-size cables as possible. One of the earlier solutions, still very widely used, is frequency division multiplexing (FDM): each of the original speech paths is modulated onto one of a specific series of radio frequency carrier waves; each such RF wave is then suppressed at the transmitting source and reinserted close to the receiving position so that only one of the sidebands (the lower), the part that actually contains the intelligence of the transmission, is actually sent over the main data path. This is similar to SSB transmission in radio.

The entire series of suppressed carrier waves are then modulated onto a further carrier wave which then becomes the main vehicle for taking the bundle of channels from one end of a line to the other. Typically, a small coaxial cable can handle 60-120 channels in this way, but large cables, the type dropped on the beds of oceans and employing several stages of modulation, can carry 2700 analog channels. Changing audio channels (as the signal leaves the telephone instrument and enters the local exchange) into RF channels, as well as making frequency division multiplexing possible, also brings benefits in that, over long circuits, it is easier to amplify RF signals to overcome losses in the cable.

Just before the Second World War, the first theoretical work was carried out to find further ways of economizing on cable usage. What was then described is called pulse code modulation – PCM. There are several stages. In the first an analog signal is sampled at specific intervals to produce a series of pulses – this is called pulse amplitude modulation and takes advantage of the characteristic of the human ear whereby, if such pulses are sent down a line with only a very small interval between them, the brain smoothes over the gaps and reconstitutes the entire original signal. In the second stage the levels of amplitude are sampled and

OPERATION OF A CHARACTER TDM

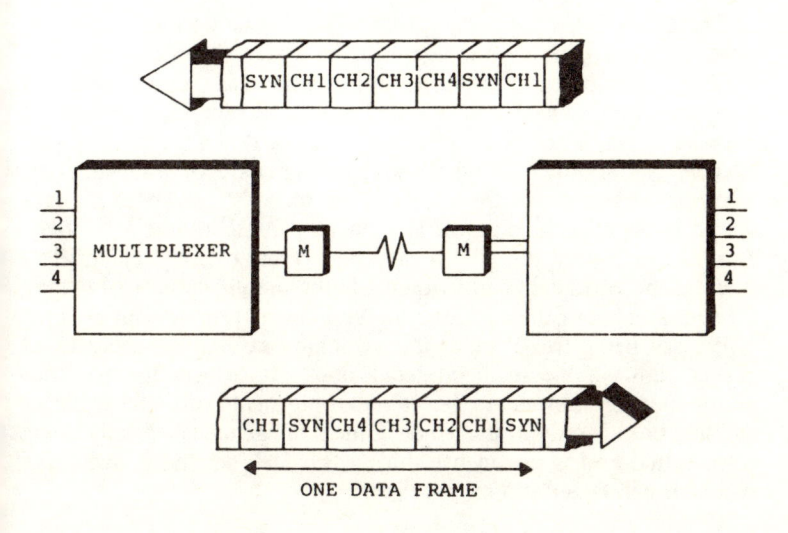

ONE DATA FRAME

translated into a binary code. The process of dividing an analog signal into digital form and then reassembling it in analog form is called quantization. Most PCM systems use 128 quantizing levels, each pulse being coded into seven binary digits, with an eighth added for supervisory purposes.

By interleaving coded characters in a high-speed digital stream it is possible to send several separate voice channels along one physical link. This process is called time division multiplexing (TDM) and together with FDM still forms the basis of most of the globe's voice-grade communications.

Digital Networks

Elegant though these solutions are – although they are rapidly being replaced by total digital schemes – they are very wasteful when all that is being transmitted are the discrete audio tones of the output of a modem. In a speech circuit the technology has to be able to 'hear' – receive, digitize and reassemble – the entire audio spectrum between 100 Hz and 3000 Hz, which is the usual pass band of what we have come to expect from the audio quality of the telephone. Moreover the technology must also be sensitive to a wide range of amplitude – speech is made up of pitch and associated loudness. In a digital network, however, all one really wants to transmit are the digits, and it doesn't matter whether they are signified by audio tones, radio frequency values, voltage conditions or light pulses, just so long as there is circuitry at either end which can encode and decode.

There are other problems with voice transmission: once two parties have made a connection with each other (by the one dialling a number and the other lifting a handset), good sense has suggested that it was desirable to keep a total physical path open between them, it not being practical to close down the path during silences and re-open it when someone speaks. In any case the electromechanical nature of most of today's phone exchanges would make such turning off and on very cumbersome and noisy. But with a purely digital transmission routing of a 'call' doesn't have to be physical – individual blocks merely have to bear an electronic label of their originating and destination addresses, such addresses being 'read' in digital switching exchanges using chips rather than in electromechanical ones. Two benefits are thus simultaneously obtained: the valuable physical path (the cable or satellite link) is only in use when some intelligence is actually being transmitted and is not in use during 'silence'; secondly, switching can be much faster and more reliable.

Packet Switching
These ideas were synthesized into creating what has now become packet switching. The methods were first described in the mid-1960s, but it was not until a decade later that suitable cheap technology existed to create a viable commercial public service. The principal British Telecom product is called Packet SwitchStream (PSS) and notable comparable US services are Compunet, Telenet and Tymnet. PSS in the UK now offers several services and there is also a young rival, run in competition by British Telecom, called Vasnet, of which more later. Many other countries have their own services and international packet switching is entirely possible – the UK service is called, unsurprisingly, IPSS.

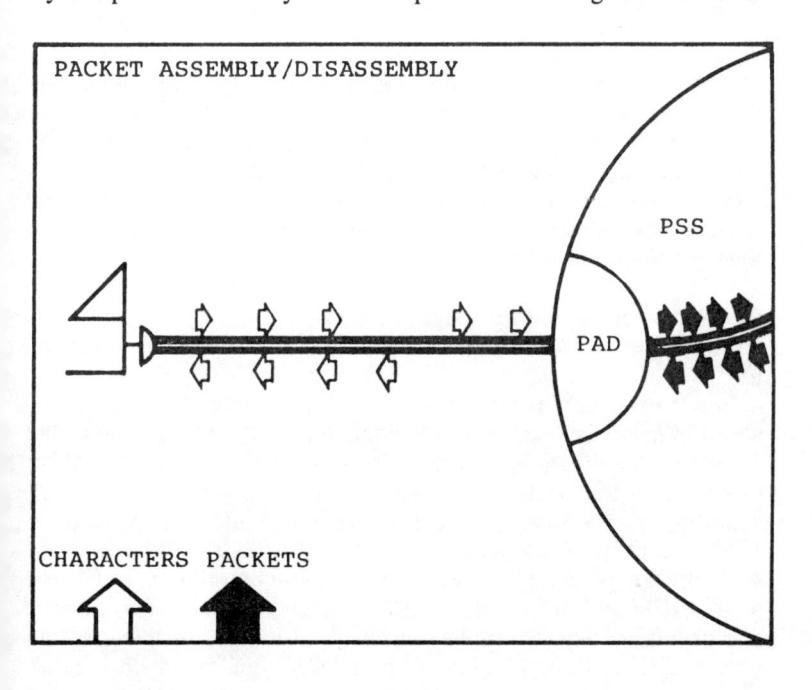

In essence the service operates at 48 kbits/s full duplex (both directions simultaneously) and uses an extension of time division multiplexing. Transmission streams are separated into convenient-sized blocks or packets, each one of which contains a head and tail signifying origination and destination. The packets are assembled, either by the originating computer or by a special facility supplied by the packet-switch system. The packets in a single transmission stream may all follow the same physical path or may use alternative routes depending on congestion. The packets from one 'conversation' are very likely to be interleaved with packets from many other 'conversations'. The originating and receiving computers see none of this. At the receiving end the various packets are stripped of their routing information and reassembled in the correct order before presentation to the computer's VDU or applications program.

All public data networks using packet switching seek to be compatible with each other, at least to a considerable degree. The international standard they have to implement is called CCITT X.25. This is a multilayered protocol covering (potentially) everything from electrical connections to the user interface.

The levels work like this:

7	Application	User interface
6	Presentation	Data formatting and code conversion
5	Session	Coordination between processes
4	Transport	Control of quality service
3	Network	Set up and maintenance of connections
2	Data link	Reliable transfer between terminal and network
1	Physical	Transfer of bitstream between terminal and network

At the moment international agreement has only been reached on the lowest three levels, Physical, Data Link and Network. Above that there is a huge galactic battle in progress between IBM, which has solutions to the problems under the name SNA (Systems Network Architecture) and most of the remainder of the principal mainframe manufacturers, whose solution is called OSI (Open Systems Interconnection).

Packet Switching and the Single User

So much for the background explanation. How does this affect the user?

Single users can access packet switching in one of two principal ways: either they use a special terminal directly able to create the data packets in an appropriate form – these are called packet terminals, in the jargon – and these sit on the packet switch circuit accessing it via the nearest PSS exchange using a permanent dataline and modems operating at speeds of 2400, 4800, 9600 or 48 kbits/s, depending on level of traffic. You can buy X.25 boards for the IBM PC, for example. Alternatively, the customer can use an ordinary asynchronous terminal, without packet-creating capabilities, and connect into a special PSS facility which handles the packet assembly for him. Such devices are called packet assembler/disassemblers, or PADs. In the jargon, such users are said to have character terminals. PADs are accessed either via leased line at 300 or 1200, or via dial-up at those speeds, but also at 1200/75.

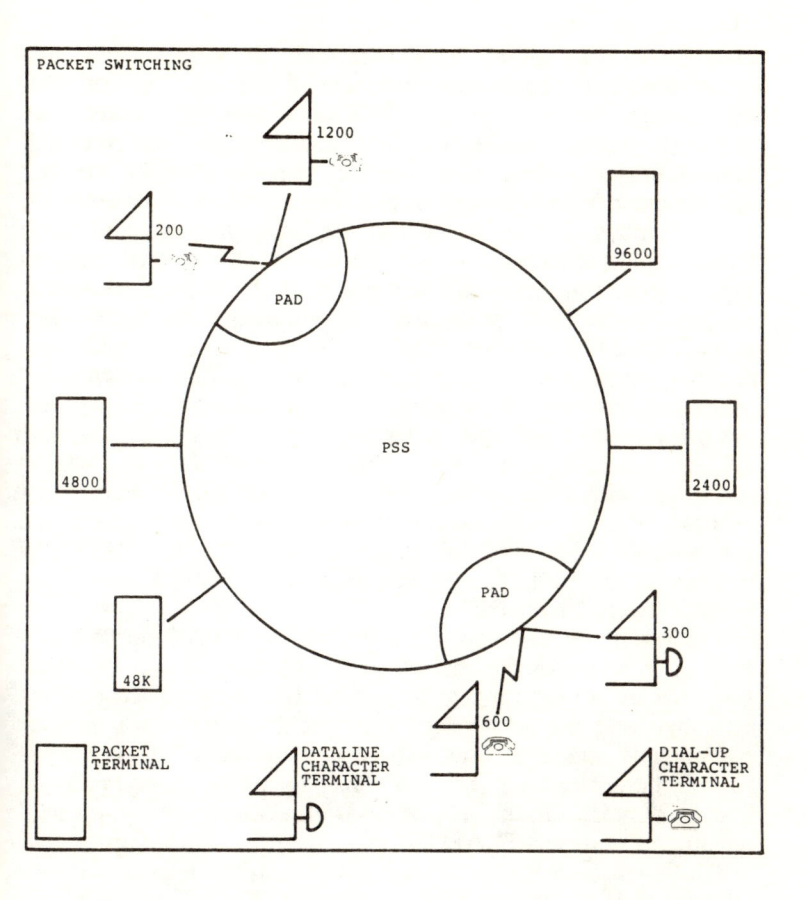

Most readers of this book, if they have used packet switching at all, will have done so using their own computers as character terminals and by dialling into a PAD. The phone numbers of UK PADs can be found in the PSS directory, published by Telecom National Networks.

In order to use PSS you as an individual need a network user identity (NUI) which is registered at your local packet switch exchange (PSE). The PAD at the PSE will throw you off if you don't give it a recognizable NUI. If you subscribe to some information services, rather than expecting you to secure your

85

own NUI, they supply you with one of their own – and incorporate the costs in their own overall charges. The UK NUI for Dialog, for example, is NDIALOG006OSQ. PADs are extremely flexible devices, they will configure their ports to suit your equipment – both as to speed and screen addressing – rather like a bulletin board (though, to be accurate, it is the bulletin board which mimics the PAD). If you are using an ordinary dumb terminal, you must send ‹cr›‹cr›A2‹cr› to tell the PAD what to expect. If you are using a a commercial VDU, the command is ‹cr›‹cr›D1‹cr›. PAD ports are available at 300 bits/s, 75/1200 and 1200/1200 full duplex. If you are using a remote information-retrieval service the most economical mode is 75/1200: the host sends you far more information than you send it, so high speed *from* the host is desirable. After all, you get four times as much information back in the same time as at 300/300 and this is important with those services that charge by time connected. If you are sending equal amounts of information, then, unless you can afford a 1200/1200 full-duplex modem (V.22), 300/300 will have to do. Do not use a viewdata emulator at 75/1200 unless you want awkward linebreaks!

The first thing that happens after dialling a PAD number and sending it details of the sort of VDU you have is that the PAD responds by transmitting to you the details of the packet-switch exchange and the number of the specific port to which your computer is attached. You then send your NUI. This is always twelve characters long. The PAD responds by echoing back the first six of these – in the case of the Dialog NUI above, you would see on your screen: NDIALOG.

The PAD then responds 'ADD?'. It wants the network user address (NUA) of the host you are calling. These are also available from the same directory: Cambridge University Computing Services's NUA is 234 222339399, BLAISE is 234 219200222, Istel is 234 252724241, and so on. The first four numbers are known as the DNIC, data network indentification code; the first three are the country – '234' is the UK identifier – and the last one the specific service in that country, '2' signifying PSS. You can also get into Prestel via PSS, though for UK purposes it is an academic exercise: A9 234 1100 2018 gives you Prestel without the graphics (A9 indicates to the system that you have a teletype terminal). Confirmation of connection comes when the full NUA is returned thus: '234222339399+COM'.

Once you have been routed to the host computer of your choice, then it is exactly if you were entering by direct dial: your password and so on will be requested.

PACKET SWITCHED NETWORK

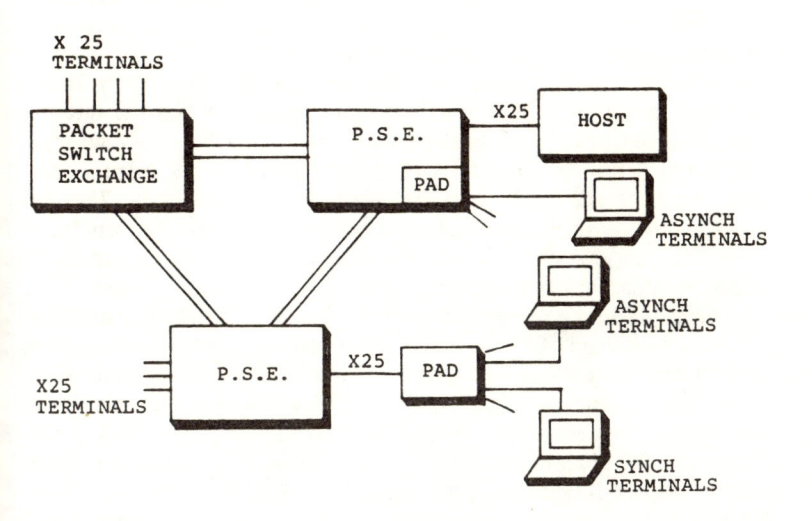

The cost of using PSS is governed by number of packets exchanged rather than the distance between two computers or the actual time of the call. A typical PSS session will thus contain the following running costs: local phone call to PAD (on regular phone bill, time-related), PSS charges (dependent on number of packets sent) and host computer bills (which could be time-related or be per record accessed or on fixed subscription).

PSS, in the form described above, is not particularly friendly to the naive user, even if some of the logging-on procedures can be installed on keyboard macros. There is one other problem: although packet switching uses error correction over its high-speed links, none used to be available between PAD and character terminal. If there was a bad line, well, tough. Accordingly, new features were introduced in 1985 under the name MultiStream. MultiStream makes it possible for a PAD to present a user with a simple menu of choices of database and/or destination. The PAD needs to be set up only once for each user. There is an option to let the user into the unfriendly world of NUAs, if necessary. So much for the user-hostility problem. Error correction is now available under the name EPAD – and it is yet another new standard to add to Xmodem, Kermit and all the existing commercial alternatives. EPAD is hardware-based, and so requires a special modem.

Finally, in recognition of the number of Prestel-compatible terminals to be found in the UK, there is a viewdata formatter called VPAD which means that owners of private videotex systems (see chapter 8) can use PSS as a national data network. However, Prestel itself doesn't use PSS.

Prestel has its own private mini-network between the various retrieval computers (the ones the public dial into) and the update and mailbox computers, and also to handle gateway connections. Prestel and Telecom Gold share (or are about to, as these words are being typed) their own network, Vasnet, named after the section of BT called Valued Added Services of which they are both part. Vasnet, for its limited purposes, is intended to be more efficient in data transmission than PSS.

There are also a number of private packet-switched networks, a few of which are limited to one large company or serve universities and research facilities, but some of which compete directly with PSS: Istel's Infotrac and ADP's Network services are two examples. Value-added networks (VANs) are basic telecoms networks or facilities to which some additional service – data processing or hosting of publishing ventures, for example – has been added.

BT also provides a number of digital communication products for large organizations outside the packet-switch system. It is up to the users of these point-to-point links to decide which protocols to use. In practice, packet-switch techniques offer the best usage of a circuit's capacity. BT's services are marketed under the name KiloStream (data rates at 2400, 4800, 9600, 48 k, 56 k – for international circuits, and 64 kbits/s) and MegaStream (even higher data rates). If you come across references to other xxxStream services, they could be: VideoStream for video conferencing, SatStream (guess), and InterStream, which provides some rather interesting gateways between services: InterStream 1 links PSS and Telex, 2 links PSS and the new high-speed telex variant teletex, 3 links teletex and telex. If you come across ADEKS or SOLENT, you have found BT services for the UK government!

Public packet switching, by offering easier and cheaper access, is a boon to the hacker. No longer does the hacker have to worry about the protocols that the host computer normally expects to see from its users. The X.25 protocol and the adaptability of the PAD mean the hacker with even lowest-quality asynchronous comms can talk to anything on the network. The tariff structure, favouring packets exchanged and not distance, means that any computer anywhere in the world can be a target. The networks are fascinating in themselves. Like most large computer installations, they have their imperfections which can be explored and exploited. And, like many systems in the process of growing to meet new challenges and markets, there are often unannounced experiments, openly available to be played with at no cost.

Austin and Poulsen, the ARPAnet hackers, made dramatic use of a private packet-switched net; the Milwaukee 414s ran around GTE's Telenet service, one of the biggest public systems in the USA. Their self-adopted name comes from the telephone area code for Milwaukee, a state chiefly known hitherto as the centre of the US beer industry.

During the spring and summer of 1983, using publicly published directories and the usual guessing games about pass numbers and passwords, the 414s dropped into the Security Pacific Bank in Los Angeles, the Sloan-Kettering Cancer Clinic in New York (it is unlikely they actually altered patients' records but merely looked at them, despite the fevered newspaper reporting of the time), a Canadian cement company and the Los Alamos Research Laboratory in New Mexico, home of the atomic bomb, and where work on nuclear weapons continues to this day. It is believed that they saw there 'sensitive' but not 'classified' files.

Commenting about their activities, one prominent computer security consultant, Joseph Coates, said, 'The Milwaukee babies are great, the kind of kids anyone would like their own to be ... There's nothing wrong with those kids. The problem is with the idiots who sold the system and the ignorant people who bought it. Nobody should buy a computer without knowing how much security is built in ... You have the timid dealing with the foolish.'

During the first couple of months of 1984 British hackers carried out a thorough exploration of SERCNET, the private packet-switched network sponsored by the Science and Engineering Research Council and centred on the Rutherford-Appleton Laboratory in Cambridge. It links together all the science and technology universities and polytechnics in the United Kingdom and has gateways to PSS and CERN (European Nuclear Research). Almost every type of mainframe and large mini-computer can be discovered hanging onto the system: IBM 3032 and 370 at Rutherford itself, Prime 400s, 550s and 750s all over the place, VAX 11/780s at Oxford, Daresbury, other VAXs at Durham, Cambridge, York, East Anglia and Newcastle, large numbers of GEC 4000 family members, and the odd PDP 11 running Unix.

Penetration was first achieved when a telephone number appeared on a popular hobbyist bulletin board, together with the suggestion that the instruction 'CALL 40' might give results. It was soon discovered that if, when asked for name and establishment, the hacker typed DEMO things started to happen. For several days hackers left one another messages on the hobbyist bulletin board, reporting progress, or the lack of it. Eventually, it became obvious that DEMO was supposed, as its name suggests, to be a limited facilities demonstration for casual users, but that it had been insecurely set up.

I can remember the night I pulled down the system manual, which had been left in an electronic file, watching page after page scroll down my VDU at 300 bits/s. All I had had to do was type the word 'GUIDE'. I remember also fetching down lists of addresses and mnemonics of SERCNET members. Included in the manual were extensive descriptions of the network protocols and their relation to 'standard' PSS-style networks.

Certain forms of access to SERCNET have since been shut off but hacker exploration continues. Another group of university-based hackers has found a similar network, JANET, rather interesting. Both networks are rather 'loose' in their structure as they were never intended for use by the naive. Gateways and interconnections appear to have been added in a very ad hoc fashion, perhaps to support particular sets of (non-computer) experimental work going on at several different centres, the results of which needed to be shared among several computer systems. Advanced hackers derive much pleasure from discovering anomalies in the networks.

Some of the best hacker stories do not have a definite ending. I offer some brief extracts from captured SERCNET sessions.

```
@3E0£8aae NODE 3.
Which Service?
PAD
COM
PAD>CALL 40
Welcome to SERCNET-PSS Gateway. Type HELP for help.

Gatewx^c!nkging in
user HELP
ID last used Wednesday, 18 January 1984 16:53
Started - Wed 18 Jan 1984 17:07:58
Please enter your name and establishment DEMO
Due to a local FTP problem, messages entered via the HELP system
during the last month have been lost. Please resubmit if problem/question
is still outstanding  9/1/84

No authorisation is required for calls which do not incur charges at the
Gateway.  There is now special support for TELEX.  A TELEX service
may be announced shortly.

Copies of the PSS Guide issue 4 are available on request to Program
Advisory Office at RAL, telephone 0235 44 6111 (direct dial in) or
0235 21900 Ext 6111.  Requests for copies should no longer be placed
in this help system.

The following options are available:
```

```
NOTES  GUIDE  TITLES  ERRORS  EXAMPLES  HELP  QUIT
Which option do you require? GUIDE
The program 'VIEW' is used to display the Gateway guide
Commands available are:
<CR> or N       next page
P               previous page
n               list page n
+n or -n        go forward or back n pages
S               first page
E               last page
L/string        find line containing string
F/string        find line beginning string
Q               exit from VIEW


VIEW Vn 6> Q
The following options are available:

NOTES  GUIDE  TITLES  ERRORS  EXAMPLES  HELP  QUIT
Which option do you require? HELP
NOTES    replies to user quries & other notes
GUIDE    is the complete Gateway user guide (including the Appendices)
TITLES   is a list of SERCNET & PSS addresses & mnemonics (Guide Appendix 1)
ERRORS   List of error codes you may receive
EXAMPLES are some examples of use of the Gateway (Guide Appendix 2)
HELP     is this
QUIT     exits from this session
The following options are available:

NOTES  GUIDE  TITLES  ERRORS  EXAMPLES  HELP  QUIT
Which option do you require? TITLES


VIEW Vn 6>

If you have any comments, please type them now, terminate with E
on a line on its own. Otherwise just type <cr>

CPU used: 2 ieu, Elapsed: 14 mins, IO: 2380 units, Breaks: 114
Budgets: this period = 32.000 AUs, used = 0.015 AUs, left = 29.161 AUs
User HELP   terminal  2 logged out  Wed 18 Jan 1984 17:21:59


 84/01/18. 18.47.00.
 I.C.C.C. NETWORK OPERATING SYSTEM.        NOS 1.1-430.20A
USER NUMBER:
PASSWORD
████████
IMPROPER LOG IN, TRY AGAIN.
USER NUMBER:
PASSWORD
>
>
>SCIENCE AND ENGINEERING RESEARCH COUNCIL
>
>RUTHERFORD APPLETON LABORATORY
>COMPUTING DIVISION
>
>
>
>
>                        The SERCNET - PSS Gateway
>
>                              User's Guide
>
>
>
>                                                              A S Dunn
>Issue 4                                                 16 February 1983
>
>
>
>
>Introduction
>
```

Frm   1; Next>
>The SERCNET-PSS Gateway provides access from SERCNET to PSS and PSS to
>SERCNET.   It functions as a 'straight through' connection between the
>networks, ie it is protocol transparant. It operates as a Transport Level
>gateway, in accordance with the 'Yellow Book' Transport Service. However
>the present implementation does not have a full Transport Service, and
>therefore there are some limitations in the service provided. For X29 which
>is incompatible with the Yellow Book Transport Service, special facilities
>are provided for the input of user identification and addresses.
>
>No protocol conversion facilities are provided by the Gateway - protocol
>conversion facilities (eg X29 - TS29) can be provided by calling through a
>third party machine (usually on SERCNET).
>
>The Transport Service addressing has been extended to include authorisation
>fields, so that users can be billed for any charges they incur.
>
>The Gateway also provides facilities for users to inspect their accounts and
>change their passwords, and also a limited HELP facility.
>
>User Interface
>
>The interface which the user sees will depend on the local equipment to
Frm   2; Next>
>which he is attached. This may be a PAD in which case he will probably be
>using the X29 protocol, or a HOST (DTE) in which case he might be using FTP
>for example. The local equipment must have some way of generating a
>Transport Service Called Address for the Gateway, which also includes an
>authorisation field - the format of this is described below. The
>documentation for the local system must therefore be consulted in order to
>find out how to generate the Transport Service Called Address. Some
>examples are given in Appendix 2.
>
>A facility is provided for the benefit of users without access to the 'Fast
>Select' facility, eg BT PAD users, (but available to all X29 terminal users)
>whereby either a minimal address can be included in the Call User Data Field
>or an X25 subaddress can be used and the Call User Data Field left absent.
>
>   - 1 -
>
>The authorisation and address can then be entered when prompted by the
>Gateway.
>
>
>Unauthorised Use
Frm   3; Next>
>.
>No unauthorised use of the Gateway is allowed regardless of whether charges
>are incurred at the Gateway or not.
>
>However, there is an account DEMO (password will be supplied on request)
>with a small allocation which is available for users to try out the Gateway,
>but it should be noted that excessive use of this account will soon exhaust
>the allocation, thus depriving others of its use.
>
>Prospective users of the Gateway should first contact User Interface Group
>in the Computing Division of the Rutherford Appleton Laboratory.
>
>
>Addressing
>
>To connect a call through the Gateway, the following information is required
>in the Transport Service Called Address:
>
>1)   The name of the called network
>2)   Authorisation, consisting of a USERID, PASSWORD and ACCOUNT, and
>   optionally, a reverse charging request
>3)   The address of the target host on the called network
Frm   4; Next>
>
>The format is as follows:
>
><netname>((<authorisation>)).<host address>
>
>
>1)   <Netname> is one of the following:

```
>SERCNET           to connect to the SERC network
>PSS               to connect to PSS
>S                 an alias for SERCNET
>69                another alias for SERCNET
>
>
>2)      <Authorisation> is a list of positional or keyword  parameters  or
>booleans as follows:
>
>Keyword           Meaning
>
>US                User identifier
>PW                User's password
>AC                the account - not used at present - taken to be same as US
Frm    5; Next>
>RP                'reply paid' request (see below)
>R                 reverse charging indicator (boolean)
>
>Keywords are separated from their values by '='.
>Keyword-value pairs, positional parameters and booleans are  separated  from
>each other by ','. The whole string is enclosed in parentheses: ().
>
>
>                                 - 2 -
>
>Examples:
>
>(FRED,XYZ,R)
>(US=FRED,PW=XYZ,R)
>(R,PW=XYZ,US=FRED)
>
>All the above have exactly the same meaning. The  first  form  is  the  most
>usual.
>
>When using positionals, the order is: US,PW,AC,RP,R
>
Frm    6; Next>
>
>3)      <Host address> is the address of the machine being called  on  the
>target network.  It may be a compound address, giving the service within the
>target machine to be used.  It may begin with a mnemonic instead of  a  full
>DTE  address.  A list of current mnemonics for both SERCNET and PSS is given
>in Appendix 1.
>
>A restriction of using the Gateway is that where a Transport Service address
>(service  name) is required by the target machine to identify the service to
>be used, then this must be included explicitly by the user in  the  Transport
>Service Called Address, and not assumed from the mnemonic, since the Gateway
>cannot know from the mnemonic, which protocol is being used.
>
>Examples:
>
>RLGB.FTP
>4.FTP
>
>Both the above would refer to the FTP service on  the  GEC  'B'  machine  at
>Rutherford.
>
>RLGB alone would in fact connect to the X29 server, since no service name is
Frm    7; Next>
>required for X29.
>
>
>In  order  to  enable  subaddresses  to  be  entered  more easily with  PSS
>addresses,  the delimiter '-' can be used to delimit a mnemonic. When  the
>mnemonic is translated to an address the delimiting '-' is deleted  so  that
>the following string is combined with the address. Eg:
>
>SERC-99 is translated to 23422351919199
>
>
>
>Putting the abovementioned three  components  together,  a  full  Transport
>Service Called Address might look like:
>
>S(FRED,XYZ,R).RLGB.FTP
```

93

>Of course a request for reverse charging on SERCNET is meaningless, but not
>illegal.
>
>Reply Paid Facility   (Omit at first reading)
>
>In many circumstances it is necessary for temporary authorisation to be
>passed to a third party. For example, the recipient of network MAIL may not
>himself be authorised to use the Gateway, and therefore the sender may wish
>to grant him temporary authorisation in order to reply. With the Job
>Transfer and Maniplulation protocol, there is a requirement to return
>output documents from jobs which have been executed on a remote site.
>
>The reply paid facility is invoked by including the RP keyword in the
>authorisation. It can be used either as a boolean or as a keyword-value
>pair. When used as a boolean, a default value of 1 is assumed.
>
>The value of the RP parameter indicates the number of reply paid calls which
>are to be authorised. All calls which use the reply paid authorisation will
>be charged to the account of the user who initiated the reply paid
>authorisation.
Frm   9; Next>
>
>The reply paid authorisation parameters are transmitted to the destination
>address of a call as a temporary user name and password in the Transport
>Service Calling Address. The temporary user name and password are in a form
>available for use by automatic systems in setting up a reply to the address
>which initiated the original call.
>
>Each time a successful call is completed using the temporary user name and
>password, the number of reply paid authorisations is reduced by 1, until
>there are none left, when no further replies are allowed. In addition there
>is an expiry date of 1 week, after which the authorisations are cancelled.
>
>In the event of call failures and error situations, it is important that the
>effects are clearly defined. In the following definitions, the term 'fail'
>is used to refer to any call which terminates with either a non-zero
>clearing cause or diagnostic code or both, regardless of whether data has
>been communicated or not. The rules are defined as follows:
>
>1)   If a call which has requested reply paid authorisation fails for any
>   reason, then the reply paid authorisation is not set up.
>
>2)   If the Gateway is unable to set up the reply paid authorisation for
Frm   10; Next>
>   any reason (eg insufficient space), then the call requesting the
>   authorisation will be refused.
>
>3)   A call which is using reply paid authorisation may not create another
>   reply paid authorisation.
>
>4)   If a call which is using reply paid authorisation fails due to a
>   network error (clearing cause non zero) then the reply paid count is
>   not reduced.
>
>5)   If a call which is using reply paid authorisation fails due to a host
>   clearing (clearing cause zero, diagnostic code non-zero) then the
>   reply paid count is reduced, except where the total number of segments
>   transferred on the call is zero (ie call setup was never completed).
>
Frm   11; Next>
>
>X29 Terminal Protocol
>
>There is a problem in that X29 is incompatible with the Transport Service.
>For this reason, it is possible that some PAD implementations will be unable
>to generate the Transport Service Called Address. Also some PAD's, eg the
>British Telecom PAD, may be unable to generate Fast Select calls - this
>means that the Call User Data Field is only 12 bytes long - insufficient to
>hold the Transport Service Address.
>
>If a PAD is able to insert a text string into the Call User Data Field,
>beginning at the fifth byte, but is restricted to 12 characters because of
>inability to generate Fast Select calls, then a partial address can be
>included, consisting of either the network name being called, or the network
>name plus authorisation.

>
>The first character is treated as a delimiter, and should be entered as the
>character '∂'. This is followed by the name of the called network - SERCNET,
>S or PSS.
>
>Alternatively, if the PAD is incapable of generating a Call User Data Field,
>then the network name can be entered as an X25 subaddress. The mechanism
Frm   12; Next>
>employed by the Gateway is to transcribe the X25 subaddress to the beginning
>of the Transport Service Called Address, converting the digits of the
>subaddress into ASCII characters in the process. Note that this means only
>SERCNET can be called with this method at present by using subaddress 69.
>
>
>The response from the Gateway will be the following message:
>
>Please enter your authorisation and address required in form:
>(user,password).address
>>
>
>Reply with the appropriate response eg:
>
>(FRED,XYZ).RLGB
>
>There is a timeout of between 3 and 4 minutes for this response, after which
>the call will be cleared. There is no limit to the number of attempts which
>may be made within this time limit - if the authorisation or address entered
>is invalid, the Gateway will request it again. To abandon the attempt, the
>call should be cleared from the local PAD.
Frm   13; Next>
>A restriction of this method of use of the Gateway is that a call must be
>correctly authorised by the Gateway before charging can begin, thus reverse
>charge calls from PSS which do not contain authorisation in the Call Request
>packet will be refused. However it is possible to include the authorisation
>but not the address in the Call Request packet. The authorisation must then
>be entered again together with the address when requested by the Gateway.
>
>The above also applies when using a subaddress to identify the called
>network. In this case the Call User Data Field will contain only the
>authorisation in parentheses (preceded by the delimiter '∂')
>
>
>_   - 5 -

>
>Due to the lack of a Transport Service ACCEPT primitive in X29, it will be
>found, on some PADs, that a 'call connected' message will appear on the
>terminal as soon as the call has been connected to the Gateway. The 'call
>connected' message should not be taken to imply that contact has been made
>with the ultimate destination. The Gateway will output a message 'Call
>connected to remote address' when the connection has been established.
>
Frm   14; Next>
>
>ITP Terminal Protocol
>
>The terminal protocol ITP is used extensively on SERCNET, and some hosts
>support only this terminal protocol. Thus it will not be possible to make
>calls directly between these hosts on SERCNET and addresses on PSS which
>support only X29 or TS29. In these cases it will be necessary to go through
>an intermediate machine on SERCNET which supports both X29 and ITP or TS29
>and ITP, such as a GEC MUM. This is done by first making a call to the GEC
>MUM, and then making an outgoing call from there to the desired destination.
>
>
>TS29 Terminal Protocol
>
>This is the ideal protocol to use through the Gateway, since there should be
>no problem about entering the Transport Service address. However, it is
>advisable first to ascertain that the machine to be called will support
>TS29.
>
>When using this protocol, the service name of the TS29 server should be
>entered explicitly, eg:

```
Frm   15; Next>
>S(FRED,XYZ).RLGB.TS29
>
>
>Restrictions
>
>Due to the present lack of a full Transport Service in the  Gateway,  some
>primitives are not fully supported.
>
>In particular, the ADDRESS, DISCONNECT and RESET primitives  are  not  fully
>supported.   However  this  should  not  present serious problems, since the
>ADDRESS and RESET  primitives  are  not  widely  used,  and  the  DISCONNECT
>primitive can be carried in a Clear Request packet.
>
>
>IPSS
>
>Access to IPSS is through PSS.  Just enter the IPSS address in place of  the
>PSS address.
>
>
```

................and on and on for 17 pages.........

8 Videotex Systems

Viewdata, or videotex as I am proposing to call it in this chapter, has had a curious history. At one stage, in the late 1970s, it was possible to believe that it was about to take over the world, giving computer power to the masses via their domestic television sets. It was revolutionary in the time it was developed, around 1975, in research laboratories owned by what was then called the Post Office but which is now British Telecom. It had a colour-and-graphics display, a user-friendly means of talking to it at a time when most computers needed precise grunts to make them work, and the ordinary layperson could learn how to use it in five minutes. The essence of videotex is that information is always presented on a 'page' or screen basis – 40 characters by 24 lines – instead of in the scrolling mode of conventional teletypewriters and VDUs. Each page always begins with a 'clear screen' command. Pages are identified by numbers rather than words and, in its original Prestel-like format, all commands use numbers only.

The videotex revolution never happened, because Prestel, its most public incarnation, was mismarketed by its owners, British Telecom, and because, in its original version, it is simply too clumsy and limited to handle more sophisticated applications. Since the information is held on electronic file cards, which can easily be either too big or too small for a particular answer, and the only way you can obtain the desired information is by keying numbers, trundling down endless indices, certain sorts of information cannot be conveniently fitted onto a videotex system without causing user fatigue. In the early days of Prestel most of what you got was indices, not substantive information. By the time that videotex sets were supposed to exist in their hundreds of thousands, home computers, not predicted at all when videotex first appeared in the mid-1970s, had already sold into the millionth British home.

Yet private videotex, minicomputers configured to look like Prestel and to use the same special terminals, has been a modest success. By mid-1985 there were over 500 significant installations in the UK. They have been set up partly to serve the needs of individual companies, but also to help particular trades, industries and professions. The falling cost of videotex terminals has made private systems attractive to the travel trade, retail stores, the motor trade, to some local authorities and the financial world. What is curious about all this is that increasingly many professional customers are using not dedicated videotex terminals but PCs with terminal emulators – the emulators reduce the number of characters displayed from 80, the norm for the IBM and Apricot sort of machine, to 40 and, graphics apart, make the machine *less* efficient as a display device!

The hacker, armed with a dumb videotex set or with a software 'fix' for his micro, can go ahead and explore these services. At the beginning of this book I said my first hack was of a videotex service, Viditel, the Dutch system. It is astonishing how many British hackers have had a similar experience. Indeed, the habit of videotex hacking has spread throughout Europe also: the wonderfully named Chaos Computer Club of Hamburg had some well-publicized fun with Bildschirmtext, the West German Prestel equivalent colloquially named Btx.

What they appear to have done was to acquire the password of the Hamburger Sparkasse, the country's biggest savings bank group. Whereas telebanking is a relatively modest part of Prestel – the service is called Homelink – the West German banks have been a powerful presence on Btx since its earliest days. In fact, another Hamburg bank, the Verbraucher Bank, was responsible for the world's first videotex gateway (see p. 102), for once in this technology showing the British the way. The twenty-five member-Chaos Computer Club probably acquired the password as a result of the carelessness of a bank employee. Having done so, they set about accessing the bank's own, rather high-priced, pages, some of which cost almost DM10 (£2.70). In a deliberate demonstration, the club then set a computer systematically to call the pages over and over again, achieving a reaccess rate of one page every 20 seconds. During a weekend in mid-November 1984 they made more than 13,000 accesses and ran up a notional bill of DM135,000 (£36,000). Information providers, of course, are not charged for looking at their own pages, so no bill was payable and the real cost of the hack was embarrassment.

In hacking terms the Hamburg hack was relatively trivial – simple password acquisition. Much more sophisticated hacks have been perpetrated by British enthusiasts.

Videotex hacking has three aspects: to break into systems and become user, editor or system manager thereof; to discover hidden parts of systems to which you have been legitimately admitted; and to uncover new services.

Videotex Software Structures

An understanding of how a videotex database is set up is a great aid in learning how to discover what might be hidden away. Remember, there are always two ways to each page – by following the internal indexes or by direct keying using *nnn*#.

In typical videotex software, each electronic file card or 'page' exists on an overall tree-like structure:

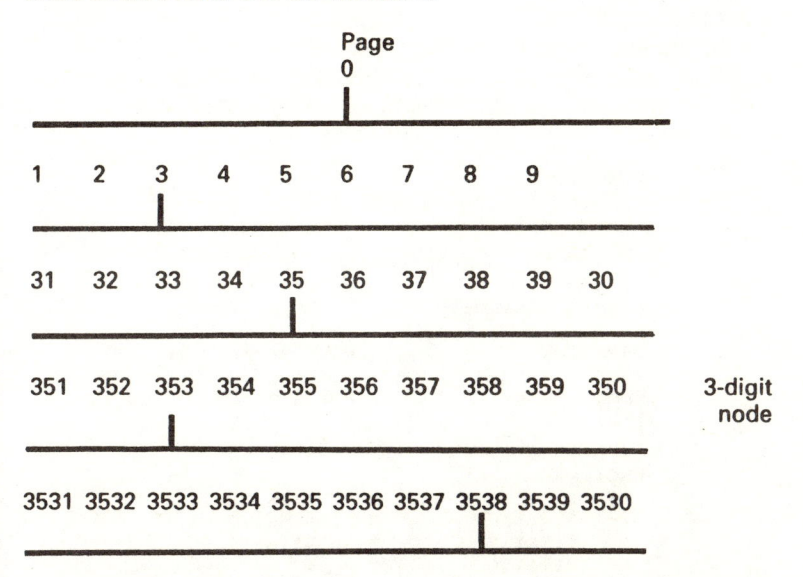

```
                           Page
                             0
─────────────────────────────┼─────────────────────────────

 1    2    3    4    5    6    7    8    9
           │
───────────┼───────────────────────────────────────────────

31   32   33   34   35   36   37   38   39   30
                    │
────────────────────┼──────────────────────────────────────

351  352  353  354  355  356  357  358  359  350      3-digit
          │                                            node
──────────┼────────────────────────────────────────────────

3531 3532 3533 3534 3535 3536 3537 3538 3539 3530
                                    │
────────────────────────────────────┼──────────────────────
```

Top pages are called parents; lower pages filials. Thus page 3538 needs parent pages 353, 35, 3 and 0 to support it, i.e. these pages must exist on the system. On Prestel, the parents owned by information providers (the electronic publishers) are three digits long (three-digit nodes). Single and double-digit pages (0 to 99) are owned by the 'system manager' (and so are any pages beginning with the sequences 100nn-199nn and any beginning with a 9nnn).

When a page is set up by an information provider (the process of going into 'edit' mode varies from software package to package; on Prestel, you call up page 910) two processes are necessary. The overt page (i.e. the display the user sees) must be written using a screen editor. Then the IP must select a series of options – for example whether the page is for gathering a response from the user or just to furnish information, whether the page is to be open for viewing by all, by a closed user group, or just by the IP (this facility is used while a large database is being written and so that users don't access part of it by mistake), the price (if any) the page

99

will bear, and the 'routing instructions'. When you look at a videotex page and it says 'Key 8 for more information on ABC', it is the routing table which is constructed during edit that tells the videotex computer 'If a user on this page keys 8, take him through to the following next page.' Thus, page 353880 may say 'More information on ABC ... KEY 8.' The information on ABC is actually held on page 3537891. The routing table on page 353880 will say: 8=3537891.

In the above example you will see that 3537891 is not a true filial of 353880 – this does not matter; however, in order for 3537891 to exist on the system, *its* parents must exist, ie there must be pages 353789, 35378, 3537, etc.

```
P R E S T E L
PRESTEL EDITING SYSTEM
 Input Details -

           Update option    o

Pageno    4190100         Frame-Id    a

User  CUG                 User access    y

Frame type    i           Frame price       2p

         Choice type    s

Choices
  0-   *              1-    4196121
  2-   4196118        3-    4196120
  4-   4196112        5-    4196119
  6-   4196110        7-    *
  8-   4190101        9-    4199
```

Prestel Editing. This is the 'choices' page which sets up the frame before the overt page – the one the user sees – is prepared.

These quirky features of videotex software can help the hacker search out hidden databases:

1 Using a published directory, you can draw up a list of 'nodes' and who occupies them. You can then list out apparent 'unoccupied' nodes and see if they contain anything interesting. It was when a hacker spotted that an 'obvious' Prestel node, 456, had been unused for a while that news first got out early in 1984 about the Prestel Microcomputing service, several weeks ahead of the official announcement.

2 If you look at the front page of a service, you can follow the routings of the main index – are all the obvious immediate filials used? If not, can you get at them by direct keying?

3   Do any services start lower down a tree than you might expect (i.e. more digits in a page number than you might have thought)? in that case, try accessing the parents and see what happens.

4   Remember that you can get a message 'no such page' for two reasons; because the page really doesn't exist, or because the information provider has put it on 'no user access'. In the latter case, check to see whether this has been done consistently – look at the immediate possible filials. To go back to when Prestel launched its Prestel Microcomputing service, using page 456 as a main node, 456 itself was closed off until the formal opening, but page 45600 was open. In fact, there are no less than three different 'no such page' messages. The first is 'MISTAKE? TRY AGAIN OR TELL US ON *36#.' The second is 'PRIVATE PAGE – FOR EXPLANATION *37#' – this indicates a page is in a closed user group. The third gives you a full-page display 'UNAVAILABLE PAGE'.

Prestel Special Features

In general this book has avoided giving specific hints about individual services, but Prestel is so widely available in the UK and so extensive in its coverage that a few generalized notes seem worthwhile:

1   Not all Prestel's databases may be found via the main index or in the printed directories; even some that are on open access are unadvertised. Of particular interest over the last few years have been nodes 640 (owned by the Research and Development team at Martlesham), 651 (Scratchpad – used for ad hoc demonstration databases), 601 (mostly mailbox facilities but also has been known to carry experimental advanced features so that they can be tried out), and 650 (news for information providers – mostly, but not exclusively in a closed user group). Occasionally equipment manufacturers offer experimental services as well: I have found high-res graphics and even instruction codes for digitized full video lurking around.

2   In theory, what you find on one Prestel computer you will find on all the others. In practice this has never been true as it has always been possible to edit individually on each computer as well as on the main updating machine which is supposed to

broadcast to all the others. The differences in what is held in each machine will become greater over time.

3 A gateway is a means of linking non-videotex external computers to the Prestel system. It enables on-screen buying and booking, complete with validation and confirmation. It even permits telebanking. There were about sixty-five external gateways on Prestel in autumn 1985. Most 'live' forms of gateway are very secure, with several layers of password and security. However, gateways require testing before they can be offered to the public; in the past hackers have been able to secure free rides out of Prestel.

4 Careful second-guessing of the routings on the databases including telesoftware* have given users free programs while the telesoftware was still being tested and before actual public release.

5 Prestel's special functions are accessible on pages *9nn#. What you can use depends on who you are. IPs, as opposed to ordinary users, get the following:

- 91   Edit facilities menu – contains facilities to frame fill response pages and convert ordinary pages into gateway frames
- 910 Edit page
- 911 CUG membership validation/devalidation
- 912 Page interrogate – to count up accesses
- 913 (Private)
- 914 Change edit password
- 92   Your Prestel bill
- 920 Change personal password

---

* Telesoftware is a technique for making regular computer programs available via videotex: the program lines are compressed according to a simple set of rules and set up on a series of videotex frames. Each frame contains a modest error-checking code. To receive a program, the user's computer, under the control of a 'download' routine, calls the first program page down from the videotex host, runs the error check on it, demands a retransmission if the check gives a 'false' or, if it gives a 'true', unsqueezes the program lines, and then dumps them into the computer's main memory or disk store. It then requests the next videotex page, and so on, until the whole program is collected. You then have a text file which must be converted into program instructions. Depending on which model of micro and which telesoftware package you have, you can either run the program immediately or 'exec' it. Personally I found the telesoftware experience interesting the first time I tried it and quite useless in terms of speed, reliability and quality ever since.

921   Thank you for changing your password
924   Programming Your Prestel set (remote facility)

93   Prestel mailbox menu
930   Display new messages
931   Display stored messages
932   Display new messages
934   Display stored messages

940   Intermediate frame leading to your welcome frame
942   Message to IPs about changes to edit passwords

970   (Private)

Prestel, so far as the ordinary user is concerned, is a very secure system – it uses fourteen-digit passwords and disconnects after three unsuccessful tries. For most purposes the only way of hacking into Prestel is to acquire a legitimate user's password, perhaps because they have copied it down and left it prominently displayed. Most commercial videotex sets allow the owner to store the first ten digits in the set (some even permit the full fourteen), thus making the casual hacker's task easier.

However, Prestel was sensationally hacked at the end of October 1984, the whole system lying at the feet of a team of West London hackers for just long enough to demonstrate the extent of their skill to a wide range of the press. Since the event has been the subject of criminal charges which are unlikely to be heard before this edition of *The Hacker's Handbook* is published, no further description or discussion can, alas, be provided.

The public Prestel service consists of a network of computers, mostly for access by ordinary users, but with two special-purpose machines, Duke, for IPs to update their information into and Pandora, to handle mailboxes (Prestel's variant on electronic mail). The computers are linked by non-public packet-switched lines. Ordinary Prestel users are registered (usually) onto two or three computers local to them which they can access with the simple three-digit telephone number 618 or 918. In most parts of the UK these two numbers will return a Prestel whistle. (BT Prestel have installed a large number of local telephone nodes and leased lines to transport users to their nearest machine at local call rates, even though in some cases that machine may be 200 miles away.) Every Prestel machine also has several regular phone numbers associated with it for IPs and engineers. Most of these numbers confer no extra privileges on callers: if you are registered to a particular computer and get in via a 'back-door' phone number you will pay Prestel and IPs exactly the same as if you had dialled 618 or 918. If you are not registered, you will be thrown off after three tries.

In addition to the public Prestel computers there are a number of other BT machines, not on the network, which look like Prestel and indeed carry versions of the Prestel database. These machines, left over from an earlier stage of Prestel's development, are now used for testing and development of new Prestel features. The old Hogarth computer, originally used for international access, is now called Gateway Test and, as its name implies, is used by IPs to try out the interconnections of their computers with those of Prestel prior to public release.

There is one relatively uncommented-upon vulnerability in the present Prestel set-up: the information on Prestel is most easily altered via the bulk update protocols used by information providers, where there is a remarkable lack of security. All the system presently requires is a four-character editing password and the IP's systel number, which is usually the same as his mailbox number (obtainable from the on-system mailbox directory on page *7#), which in turn is very likely to be derived from a phone number. This loophole should soon be closed.

Other Videotex Services

A large number of other videotex services exist: in addition to the Stock Exchange's TOPIC and the other videotex based services mentioned in chapter 4, the travel trade has really clutched the technology to its bosom. The typical high street agent not only accesses Prestel but several other services – in some cases as many as eleven – which give up-to-date information on the take-up of holidays, announce price changes and allow confirmed airline and holiday bookings.

Several of the UK's biggest car manufacturers have a stock locator system for their dealers. If you want a British Leyland model with a specific range of accessories and in the colour combination of your choice, the chances are that your local dealer will not have it stock. He can, however, use the stock locator to tell him with which other dealer such a machine may be found. Other motor vehicle systems are run by BMW, Fiat, Ford, General Motors (Vauxhall-Opel), Mazda, Talbot (the system is called VITAL), Volvo, VW-Audi (VAG Dialog), and Yamaha runs a videotex service for its motorcycle dealers. Secondhand dealers can use Gladiator to check up on prices – it is based on the well-known *Glass's Guide* – FACT to discover recent car auction prices and Viewtrade for inter-dealer trading.

Stock control and management information is used by retail chains using, in the main, a package developed by a subsidiary of Debenhams. Debenhams had been early enthusiasts of Prestel in the days when it was still being pitched at a mass consumer audience – its service was called Debtel, which wags suggested was for people who owed money. Later it formed DISC to link together its retail outlets and this was hacked in 1983. The store denied that anything much had happened, but the hacker appeared (in shadow) on a TV programme together with a quite convincing demonstration of his control over the system. Rumbelows and BHS are also videotex enthusiasts, Littlewoods have ShopTV on Prestel – a gateway ordering service; and Tesco have been running a home ordering facility for the housebound in the Gateshead area for some time. A similar service in London comes from Telecard.

The Press Association provides a news digest called Newsfile – it is mostly used by the public relations industry and has an economics digest service called Esmark. Audience research data is despatched in videotex mode to advertising agencies and broadcasting stations by AGB Market Research.

Local authorities in the UK have also clasped videotex to their bosoms. As well as the umbrella bureau service, Laser, the following are all owners of private videotex systems of various sizes: Basildon, Berkshire, Birmingham, Gateshead, Gloucestershire, Hackney, Herts (the pioneer and the first private system I hacked into – see chapter 6), Kent, Kingston-on-Thames (it's called Kingtel, I'm afraid), Milton Keynes (Milton Skreens, ugh), Northamptonshire, North Herts, Oxfordshire and Suffolk. There are a number of other experiments, some of them using nothing more extensive than BBC micros running CommunItel software – a package much favoured by the ITECs, incidentally.

There are also databases, often using CommunItel, which are halfway between commercial services and bulletin boards. Some are used simply to record out-of-hours requests for mail-order houses, but some, like that run by the Radio Society of Great Britain for radio amateurs, carries substantive news and features.

Beyond this there are alternate videotex networks rivalling that owned by Prestel, the most important of which is, at the time of writing, the one run by Istel and headquartered at Redditch in the Midlands. This service, called Viewshare, sits on Istel's Infotrac network and claims to be the world's largest videotex service, larger than Prestel. It transports several different trade and professional services as well as the internal data of BL, of which Istel is a subsidiary. Another network is called Viewdata Gold and is run by Air Call plc.

A videotex *front-end processor* is a minicomputer package which sits between a conventionally-structured database and its ports which look into the phone lines. Its purpose is to allow users with videotex sets to search the main database without having to purchase an additional conventional dumb terminal. Some videotex front-end processors (FEPs) expect the user to have a full alphabetic keyboard and merely transform the data into videotex pages 40 characters by 24 lines in the usual colours. More sophisticated FEPs go further and allow users with only numeric keypads to retrieve information as well. By using FEPs a database publisher or system provider can reach a larger population of users. FEPs have been known to have a lower standard of security protection than the conventional systems to which they were attached.

Many of the private viewdata services described above are run on FEPs rather than Prestel-like software packages. As a result they are likely to have such un-Prestel-like features as keyword access − try typing *HELP#, which is nearly always in any keyword thesaurus. ICC (InterCompany Comparisons) have a very slick videotex service − see chapter 4 − which is easier and cheaper to use than the same database on Dialog. A particularly impressive service comes from the credit agency CCN − again chapter 4 has the details.

The careful videotex hacker soon gets to recognize the dominant software packages used on mainframes from the format of the sign-on page to the differences in page header design and 'command pages'. Prestel-like services, as noted, used *90# to log off; others use *04# or some such. The packages you'll see over and over again are Aregon's IVS-3, Computex, ICL Bulletin and Mistel. Each has its own characteristic command set to access editing and system manager functions. See if they work even if they are not clearly listed on the main menus of the service.

Videotex Standards

The UK videotex standard − the particular graphics set and method of transmitting frames − is adopted in many other European countries and in former UK imperial possessions. Numbers and passwords to access these services occasionally appear on bulletin boards and the systems are particularly interesting to enter while they are still on trial. As a result of a quirk of Austrian law, anyone can legitimately enter their service without a password, although one is needed if you are to extract valuable information. However, important variants to the UK standards exist. The French (inevitably) have a system that is remarkably similar in outline but incompatible. In North America the emerging standard which was originally put together by the Canadians for their Telidon service, but which has now, with modifications, been promoted by Ma Bell, has high-resolution graphics because, instead of building up images from block graphics, it uses picture description techniques (e.g. draw line, draw arc, fill in, etc.) of the sort relatively familiar to most users of modern home micros. Implementations of NAPLPS (as the US standard is called) are available for the IBM PC.

The Finnish public service uses software which can handle nearly all videotex formats, including a near photographic mode. Software similar to that used in the Finnish public service – Mistel – can be found on some private systems.

Countries vary considerably in their use of videotex technology: the German and Dutch systems consist almost entirely of gateways to third-party computers; the French originally justified the cost of their system by linking it to a massive project to make all telephone directories open to electronic inquiry, thus saving the cost of printed versions. French videotex terminals thus have full alpha keyboards instead of the numbers-only versions common in other countries. For the French the telephone directory is central and all other information peripheral. Teletel/Antiope, as the service is called, suffered its first serious hack late in 1984 when a journalist on the political/satirical weekly *Le Canard Enchaîné* claimed to have penetrated the Atomic Energy Commission's computer files accessible via Teletel and uncovered details of laser projects, nuclear tests in the South Pacific and an experimental nuclear reactor.

Videotex: The Future

Videotex grew up at a time when the idea of mass computer ownership was a fantasy, when the idea that private individuals could store and process data locally was considered farfetched, and when there were fears that the general public would have difficulties in tackling anything more complicated than a numbers-only keypad. These failures of prediction have lead to the limitations and clumsiness of present-day videotex. Nevertheless, the energy and success of the hardware salesmen, plus the reluctance of companies and organizations to change their existing set-ups, will ensure that for some time to come, new private videotex systems will continue to be introduced ... and be worth trying to break into.

There is one dirty trick that hackers can perform on many

private videotex systems. Entering them is often easy because high-level editing passwords are, as mentioned earlier, sometimes desperately insecure (see chapter 6) and it is easy to acquire editing status.

What you do, once you have discovered you are an editor, is to go to edit mode. You then edit the first page on the system, page 0; you can usually place your own message on it, of course; but you can also default all the routes to page 90. Now *90# in Prestel-like videotex systems is the log-out command, so the effect is that, as soon as someone logs in successfully and tries to go beyond the first page, the system logs them out. However, this is no longer a new trick and one which should be used with caution – is the database used by an important organization? Are you going to tell the system manager what you have done and urge more care in password selection in future?

9 Radio Computer Data

Vast quantities of data traffic are transmitted daily over the radio frequency spectrum; hacking is simply a matter of hooking up a good-quality radio receiver and a computer through a suitable interface. On offer are news services from the world's great press agencies, commercial and maritime messages, meteorological data, and plenty of heavily encrypted diplomatic and military traffic. The press agency material is a back-up for land-line-based services or for those going through satellites. A variety of systems, protocols and transmission methods are in use and the hacker jaded by land-line communication (and perhaps for the moment put off by the cost of phone calls) will find plenty of fun on the airwaves.

In the first edition of this book I gave a swift overview of radio hacking; it is clear from the letters I received that this subject was more of a novelty and more interesting to readers than I had assumed. Accordingly, I have expanded the chapter and now include material on satellites.

The techniques of radio hacking are similar to those necessary for computer hacking. Data transmission over the airwaves usually uses either a series of audio tones to indicate binary 0 and 1, which are modulated on transmit and demodulated on receive, or alternatively frequency-shift keying, which involves the sending of one of two slightly different radio frequency carriers, corresponding to binary 0 or binary 1. The two methods of transmission sound identical on a communications receiver (see below) and both are treated the same for decoding purposes. The tones are different from those used on land lines: 'space' is nearly always 1275 Hz and 'mark' can be one of three tones – 1445 Hz (170 Hz shift – quite often used by amateurs and with certain technical advantages), 1725 Hz (450 Hz shift – the one most commonly used by commercial and news services) and 2125 Hz (850 Hz shift – also used commercially). There are other radio transmissions which use tones, but not in this way. These include the piccolo system which uses thirty-two tones and another, much favoured for UK military long-haul work, which uses up to twenty-four tones. Such transmissions, which are parallel rather than serial, require ultra-stable receivers even before you attempt to work out what is really going on!

The commonest two-tone protocol uses the 5-bit Baudot code rather than 7-bit or 8-bit ASCII. The asynchronous, start/stop mode is the most common. Transmission speeds include: 45 bits/s (60 words/minute), 50 bits/s (66 words/minute), 75 bits/s (100 words/minute). 50 bits/s is the most common. However, many interesting variants can be heard – special versions of Baudot for non-European languages, and error-correction protocols.

The material of greatest interest is to be found in the high-frequency or 'short-wave' part of the radio spectrum, which goes from 2 MHz, just above the top of the medium-wave broadcast band, through to 30 MHz, which is the far end of the 10 metre amateur band, which itself is just above the well-known Citizens' Band at 27 MHz.

The reason this section of the spectrum is so interesting is that, unique among radio waves, it has the capacity for worldwide propagation without the use of satellites, the radio signals being bounced back, in varying degrees, by the ionosphere. This special quality means that *everyone* wants to use HF (high-frequency) transmission – not only international broadcasters, the propaganda efforts of whom are the most familiar uses of HF. Data transmission certainly occurs on all parts of the radio spectrum, from VLF (very low frequency, the portion below the long wave broadcast band which is used for submarine communication), through the commercial and military VHF and UHF bands, beyond SHF (super-high frequency, just above 1000 MHz), right to the microwave bands. But HF is the most rewarding in terms of range of material available, content of messages and effort required to access it.

Before going any further, hackers should be aware that in a number of countries even *receiving* radio traffic for which you are not licensed is an offence; in nearly all countries *making* use of information so received is also an offence and, in the case of news-agency material, breach of copyright may also present a problem. However, owning the equipment required is usually not illegal and, since few countries require a special licence to *listen* to amateur radio traffic (as opposed to transmitting, in which case a licence is needed) and since amateurs transmit in a variety of data modes as well, hackers can set about acquiring the necessary capability without fear.

Equipment
The equipment required consists of a communications receiver, an

antenna, an interface unit/software and a computer.

Communications receiver This is the name given to a good-quality high-frequency receiver. Suitable models can be obtained, secondhand, at around £100; new receivers cost upwards of £175. There is no point in buying a radio simply designed to pick up short-wave broadcasts – they will lack the sensitivity, selectivity and resolution necessary. A minimum specification would be:

coverage	500 kHz-30 MHz
resolution	›100 Hz
modes	AM, upper side band, lower side Band, CW (Morse)

Tuning would be either by two knobs, one for MHz, one for kHz, or by keypad. On more expensive models it is possible to vary the bandwidth of the receiver so that it can be widened for musical fidelity and narrowed when listening to bands with many signals close to one another.

Broadcast stations transmit using AM – amplitude modulation – but in the person-to-person contacts of the aeronautical, maritime and amateur world, single-sideband suppressed-carrier techniques are used – the receiver will feature a switch marked AM, USB, LSB, CW, etc. Sideband transmission uses less frequency space and so allows more simultaneous conversations to take place, and is also more efficient in its use of the power available at the transmitter. The chief disadvantage is that equipment for receiving is more expensive and must be more accurately tuned. Upper sideband is used on the whole for voice traffic and lower sideband for data traffic. (Radio amateurs are an exception: they also use lower sideband for voice transmissions below 10 MHz.)

Suitable sources of supply for communications receivers are amateur radio dealers, whose addresses may be found in specialist magazines like *Practical Wireless, Amateur Radio, Ham Radio Today.*

Antenna Antennas are crucial to good shortwave reception – the sort of short 'whip' aerial found on portable radios is quite insufficient if you are to capture transmissions from across the globe. When using a computer close to a radio you must also take considerable care to ensure that interference from the CPU and monitor don't squash the signal you are trying to receive. The sort of antenna I recommend is the 'active dipole', which has the twin advantages of being small and of requiring little operational attention. It consists of a couple of 1-metre lengths of wire tied parallel to the ground and meeting in a small plastic box. This is mounted as high as possible, away from interference, and is the 'active' part. From the plastic box descends coaxial cable which is brought down to a small power supply next to the receiver and from there the signal is fed into the receiver itself. The plastic box contains special low-noise transistors.

It is possible to use simple lengths of wire but these usually operate well only on a limited range of frequencies and you will need to cover the entire HF spectrum.

Active antennas can be obtained by mail order from suppliers advertising in amateur radio magazines – the Datong is highly recommended.

Interface
The 'interface' is the equivalent of the modem in land-line communications; indeed, advertisements of newer products actually refer to radio modems. Radio teletype, or RTTY, as it is called, is traditionally received on a modified teleprinter or telex machine and the early interfaces or terminal units (TUs) simply converted the received audio tones into 'mark' and 'space' to act as the equivalent of the electrical line conditions of a telex circuit.

Since the arrival of the microcomputer, however, the design has changed dramatically and the interface now has to perform the following functions:

1 Detect the designated audio tones.
2 Convert them into electrical logic states.
3 Strip the start/stop bits, convert the Baudot code into ASCII equivalents, reinsert start/stop bits.
4 Deliver the new signal into an appropriate port on the computer. (If RS232C is not available, then any other port – e.g. user interface or game – that is.)

A large number of designs exist. Some consist of hardware interfaces plus a cassette, disk or ROM for the software; others contain both the hardware for signal acquisition and firmware for its decoding in one box. In selecting a design, pay particular attention to the supplied tuning device; at the very least you should have two LEDs to indicate 'mark' and 'space'. More advanced devices feature a LED bargraph; topnotch professional boxes have a small cathode-ray tube display.

Costs vary enormously and do not always appear to be related to quality of result. The kit builder with a ZX Spectrum can have a complete set-up for under £40; semiprofessional models, including keyboards and screen can cost in excess of £1000.

Until recently the kit I used was based on the Apple II (because of that model's great popularity in the USA, much hardware and software exist); the interface talks into the game port and I have several items of software to present Baudot, ASCII or Morse at will. There is even some interesting software for the Apple which needs no extra hardware – the audio from the receiver is fed direct into the cassette port of the Apple, but this method is difficult to replicate on other machines because of the Apple's unique method of reading data from cassette.

I now use a full-feature radio modem (exactly the same size as my principal phone modem, as it happens) which contains a sophisticated firmware set. I simply feed audio tones into it and 7-bit ASCII at 300 baud at RS232C levels comes out. I can command it with the same software package I use down the phone lines. The firmware copes with Baudot and Morse at all reasonable speeds, ASCII transmissions and the error-correcting protocol, AMTOR, of which more later. Used in association with a transmitter, it will also originate radio data as well. Secondhand, it cost less than £200.

Excellent inexpensive hard/firmware is available for many Tandy computers and also for the VIC20/Commodore 64. On the whole US suppliers seem better than those in the UK or Japan – products are advertised in the US magazines *QST* and *73*. In the UK you should look in the same amateur radio magazines as for receivers. *RadCom*, the magazine of the Radio Society of Great Britain (RSGB), often has interesting software in the classified section at the back and is a good source of secondhand equipment.

Setting Up
Particular attention should be paid to linking all the equipment together; there are special problems about using sensitive radio receiving equipment in close proximity to computers and VDUs. Computer logic blocks, power supplies and the synchronizing pulses on VDUs are all excellent sources of radio interference (RFI). RFI appears not only as individual signals at specific points on the radio dial but also as a generalized hash which can blank out all but the strongest signals. Interference can escape not only from poorly packaged hardware but also from unshielded cables which act as aerials.

The remedy is simple to describe: encase and shield everything, connecting all shields to a good earth, preferably one separate from the mains earth. In practice, much attention must be paid to the detail of the interconnections and the relative placing of items of equipment. In particular, the radio's aerial should use coaxial feeder with a properly earthed outer braid so that the actual wires that pluck the signals from the ether are well clear of computer-created RFI. It is always a good idea to provide a communications receiver with a proper earth, although it will work without one; if used with a computer it is essential. Plastic-cased computers cause particular problems – get a metal case or line the inside with cooking foil; if you do the latter, be careful to avoid shortcircuits and watch out you don't deny the circuit board air circulation or your computer will overheat!

Do not let these paragraphs put you off; with care excellent results can be obtained. And bear in mind my own first experience: ever eager to try out some new kit, I banged everything together with great speed – ribbon cable, poor solder joints, an antenna taped quickly to a window in a metal frame less than 2 metres from the communications receiver – and all I could hear from 500 kHz to 30 MHz, wherever I tuned, was a great howl whine of protest.

Where to Listen

Scanning through the bands on a good communications receiver, you realize just how crowded the radio spectrum is. The table in appendix VII gives you an outline of the sandwich-like fashion in which the bands are organized.

The 'fixed' bands are the ones of interest; more particularly, the following ones are where you could expect to locate news agency transmissions (in kHz):

3155– 3400	14350–14990
3500– 3900	15600–16360
3950– 4063	17410–17550
4438– 4650	18030–18068
4750– 4995	18168–18780
5005– 5480	18900–19680
5730– 5950	19800–19990
6765– 7000	20010–21000
7300– 8195	21850–21870
9040– 9500	22855–23200
9900– 9995	23350–24890
10100–11175	25010–25070
11400–11650	25210–25550
12050–12330	26175–28000
13360–13600	29700–30005
13800–14000	

In addition, amateurs tend to congregate around certain spots on the frequency map: 3950, 14090, 21090 and 28090; and at VHF/UHF: 144.600, 145.300, 432.600, 433.300.

Radio stations do not always observe band plans, unfortunately. For the last few years propagation conditions on the HF bands have been poor. What has been happening is that the ionosphere has temporarily lost some of its capacity to reflect back radio waves – we are currently in the trough of the eleven-year sunspot cycle. As a result the higher frequencies have been useless for international radio communication and everyone, *all* users of the HF spectrum, have crowded into the few available megahertz.

Some of the bulletin boards cover radio material; you could find propagation reports and, in the hacking sections, details of individual frequencies.

Many of the more important radio services transmit on more than one frequency simultaneously (the same is true of international broadcasts). This is to maximize their chance of being heard, even in poor propagation conditions. Professional receivers listen on two or more frequencies simultaneously and a 'black box' picks the strongest signal out from moment to moment – this is called diversity reception.

The generally received opinion in the UK is that it is unwise to publish frequency lists. However, useful overseas publications can be obtained by mail order or in some amateur radio outlets. The best-known US titles are the Gilfer *Guide to RTTY Frequencies* and *Confidential Frequency List*, but they cover what can be heard in North America as opposed to Europe. In many US electronics stores you will also find directories of local VHF and UHF 'utility' services – police, ambulance, paramedic, forestry, customs, dispatch services, etc. These are for use with VHF/UHF scanners; don't buy them by mistake. The best openly available frequency lists are produced by a one-man firm called Klingenfuss. He produces an annual *Utility Guide* as well as subsidiary books covering variants on standard Baudot – third shift Amharic and Thai, two versions of Cyrillic RTTY, Arabic and Japanese formats, and the special codes used in meteorological services. Klingenfuss is expensive but worthwhile. His address is Panoramastrasse 81, D-7400 Tübingen, Federal Repulic of Germany.

Tuning In

Radio teletype signals have a characteristic two-tone warble sound which you will only hear properly if your receiver is operating in SSB (single sideband) mode. There are other digital tone-based signals to be heard, FAX (facsimile), Hellschreiber (which uses a technique similar to dot-matrix printers and is used for Chinese and related pictogram-style alphabets), SSTV (slow-scan television, which can take up to 8 seconds to send a low-definition picture), piccolo, and others. But with practice the particular sound of RTTY can easily be recognized. More experienced listeners can also identify shifts and speeds by ear.

You should tune into the signal watching the indicators on your terminal unit to see that the tones are being properly captured — typically this involves getting two LEDs to flicker simultaneously. The software will now try to decode the signal and it will be up to you to set the speed and 'sense'. The first speed to try is 66/7 words/minute, which corresponds to 50 bits/s, as this is the most common. On the amateur bands the usual speed is 60 words/minute (45 bits/s); thereafter, if the rate sounds unusually fast you try 100 words/minute (approximately 75 bits/s). By 'sense' or 'phase' is meant whether the higher tone corresponds to logical 1 or logical 0. Services can use either format, indeed the same transmission channel may use one 'sense' on one occasion and the reverse 'sense' on another. Your software or firmware can usually cope with this. If it can't all is not lost: you retune your receiver to the opposite sideband and the phase will thereby be reversed. So if you are listening on the lower sideband (LSB), usually the conventional way to receive, you simply switch over to USB (upper sideband), retune the signal into the terminal unit, and the 'sense' will have been reversed.

Many news agency stations try to keep their channels open even if they have no news to put out: usually they do this by sending test messages like: 'The quick brown fox ... ' or sequences like 'RYRYRYRYRYRY ...'. Such signals are useful for testing purposes, even if after a while they are a little dull to watch scrolling up the VDU screen.

You will discover many signals that you can't decode: the commonest reason is that the transmissions do not use European alphabets and that all the elements in the Baudot code have been reassigned — some versions of Baudot use not two shifts but three, to give the required range of characters. Klingenfuss describes ways in which you can use conventional Baudot software to work out which language is being used and to guess what the transmission is about. Straightforward encrypted messages are usually recognizable as coming in groups of five letters, but the encryption can also operate at the bit as well as the character level — in that case, too, you will get gobbledegook.

A limited amount of ASCII, as opposed to Baudot, code is to be found, but mostly on the amateur bands.

Finally, an error-correction protocol, called SITOR, is increasingly to be found on the maritime bands, with AMTOR, an amateur variant, on the amateur bands. SITOR has various modes of operation but, in its fullest implementation, messages are sent in blocks which must be formally acknowledged by the recipient before the next one is dispatched. The transmitter keeps trying until an acknowledgement is received. The process is very similar to that used in Xmodem. You may even come across, on the amateur bands, packet radio, which has many of the features of packet switching on digital land lines. This is one of the latest enthusiasms in amateur radio with at least two different protocols in relatively wide use. The one more likely to succeed is called, for obvious reasons, AX.25. Discussion of SITOR and packet radio is beyond the scope of this book, but the reader is referred to BARTG, the British Amateur Radio Teletype Group, and its magazine *Datacom*, for further information. You do not need to be a licensed radio amateur to join.

Operational problems of radio hacking are covered at the end of appendix I, the Baudot code is given appendix IV and an outline frequency plan is to be found in appendix VII.

Computer Control of Radios

The latest generation of receivers for the amateur market feature computer interfaces: frequency and mode selection can be executed from a remote computer. A radio service could be called up by name, as opposed to by frequency. Where a transmission occurs on several frequencies simultaneously, the program could check which was being received best or could calculate which frequency was *likely* to be best, based on predictions about propagation conditions. As home micros become able to support multitasking, I expect to see programs which both command radios and decode their traffic – an amateur GCHQ or NSA!

The material that follows represents some of the types of common transmissions: news services, test slips (essentially devices for keeping a radio channel open) and amateur. The corruption in places is due either to poor radio propagation conditions or to the presence of interfering signals.

```
REVUE DE LA PRESSE ITALIENNE DU VENDREDI 28 DECEMBR
E 1984
;;;;;;;;;;;;;;;;;;;;;;;;;;;;;;;;;;;;;;;;;;;;;;;;;;;

    LE PROCES AUX ASSASSINS DE L-\\3 POIELUSZKO, LA VISITE DE
M. SPADOLINI A ISRAEL, LA SITUATION AU CAMBODGE ET LA GUER-
ILLA AU MOZAMBIQUE FONT LES TITES DES PAGES POLITIQUES
```

MOBILISATION TO WORK FOR THE ACCOUNT OF 1985

- AT THE ENVER HOXHA AUTOMOBILE AND
TRACTOR COMBINE IN TIRANA 2

TIRANA, JANUARY XATA/. - THE WORKING PEOPLE OF THE ENVER HOXH
AUTOMOBILE AND TRACTOR COMBINE BEGAN THEIR WORK WITH VIGOUR
AND MOBILISATION FOR THE ACCOUNT OF 1985. THE WORK IN THIS
IMPROVOWNT CENTER FOR MECHANICAL INDUSTRY WAS NOT INTERRUPTED
FOR ONE MOMENT AND THE WORKING PEOPLE 83$ ONE ANOTHER FOR
FRESHER GREATER VICTORIES UNDER THE LEADERSHIP OF THE PARTY
WITH ENVER HOXHA AT THE HEAD, DURING THE SHIFTS, NEAR
THE FURNACES, PRESSES ETC.. JUST LIKE SCORES OF WORKING COLLE-
CTIVES OF THE COUNTRY WHICH WERE NOT AT HOME DURING THE NEW
YEAR B
A
IN THE FRONTS OF WORK FOR THE BENEFITS OF THE SOCI-
ALIST CONSTRUCTION OF THE COUNTRY.
 PUTTING INTO LIFE THE TEACHINGS OF THE PARTY AND THE INSTRU-
CTIONS OF COMRADE ENVER HOXHA, THE WORKING COLLECTIVE OF THIS
COMBINE SCORED FRESH SUCCESSES DURING 1984 TO REALIZE THE
INDICES OF THE STATE PLAN BY RASING THE ECEONOMIC EFFECTIVE-
NESS. THE WORKING PEOPLE SUCCESSFULLY REALIZED AND OVERFUL
FILLED THE OBJECTIVE OF THE REVOLUTIONARY DRIVE ON THE HIGHER
EFFECTIOVENESS OF PRODUCTION, UNDERTAKEN IN KLAIDQAULSK SO,
WITHIN 1984 THE PLANNED PRODUCTIVITY, ACCORDING TO THE INDEX
OF THE FIVE YEAR PLAN, WAS OVERFULFILLED BY 2 PER CENT.
MOREOVER, THE FIVE YEAR PLAN FOR THE GMWERING OF THE COST OF
PRODUCTION WAS RAISED 2 MONTHS AHEAD OF TIME, ONE FIVE YEAR
PLAN FOR THE PRODUCTION OF MACHINERIES LAND EQUIPMENT AND
THE PRODUCTION OF THE TRACTORS WAS OVER-
FULFILLED. THE NET INCOME OF THE FIVE YEAR PLAN WAS REALIZED
WITHIN 4 YEARS. ETCM

RYRYRYRYRYRYRYRYRYRYRYRYRYRYRYRYRYRYRYRYRYRYRYRYRYRYRYRYRYRY
YRYRYRYRYRYRYRYRYRYRYRYRYRYRYRYRYRYRYRYRYRYRYRYRYRYRYRYRYRYR
RYRYRYRYRYRYRYRYRYRYRYRYRYRYRYRYRYRYRYRYRYRYRYRYRYRYRYRYRYRY
RYRYRYRYRYRYRYRYRYRYRYRYRYRYRYRYRYRYRYRYRYRYRYRYRYRYRYRYRYRY
RYRYRYRYRYRYRYRYRYRYRYRYRYRYRYRYRYRYRYRYRYRYRYD DE GJ4YAD
GJ4YAD GJ4YAD DE G4DF G4DF
SOME QRM BUT MOST OK. THE SHIFT IS NORMAL...SHIFT IS NORMAL.
FB ON YOUR RIG AND NICE TO MEET YOU IN RTTY. THE WEATHER HERE
TODAY IS FINE AND BEEN SUNNY BUT C9LD. I HAVE BEEN IN THIS MOD
BEFORE BUT NOT FOR A FEW YEARS HI HI.

GJ4YAD GJ4YAD DE G4DF G4DF
PSE KKK

G4EJE G4EJE DE G3IMS G3IMS
TNX FOR COMING BACK. RIG HERE IS ICOM 720A BUT I AM SENDING
AFSK NOT FSK. I USED TO HAVE A CREED BUT CHUCKED IT OUT IT WAS

```
TOO NOISY AND NOW HAVE VIC20 SYSTEM AND SOME US KIT MY SON
BROUGHT ME HE TRAVELS A LOT.
HAD LOTS OF TROUBLE WITH RFI AND HAVE NOT YET CURED IT. VERTY BAD
QRM AT MOMENT. CAN GET NOTHING ABOVE 10 MEGS AND NOT MUCH EX-G ON
80. HI HI. SUNSPOT COUNT IS REALLY LOW.

G4EJE G4EJE DE G3IMS G3IMS
KKKKKKKKKKK
RYRYRYRYRYRYRYRYRYR
KKKKKKKKKKK


G3IMS G3IMS DE G4EJE G4EJE
FB OM. QRM IS GETTING WORSE. I HAVE ALWAYS LIKED ICOM RIGS BUT
THEY ARE EXEPENSIVE. CAN YOU RUN FULL 100 PER CENT DUTY CYCLE ON
RTTY OR DO YOU HAVE TO RUN AROUND 50 PER CENT. I GET OVER-HEATING
ON THIS OLD YAESU 101. WHAT SORT OF ANTENNA SYSTEM DO YOU USE.
HERE IS A TRAPPED VERTICAL WITH 80 METERS TUNED TO RTTY SPOT AT
3590.
I STILL USE CREED 7 THOUGH AM GETTING FED UP WITH MECHANICAL
BREAK-DOWN AND NOISE BUT I HAVE HEARD ABOUT RFI AND HOME
COMPUTERS. MY NEPHEW HAS A SPECTRUM, CAN YOU GET RTTY SOFTWARE
FOR THAT/.

G3IMS G3IMS DE G4EJE G4EJE
PSE KKK
```

Satellites

With rather different receiving equipment and a rather different antenna system, it is possible to eavesdrop on data traffic carried on satellites. There are three types which can be easily heard: amateur satellites, educational satellites and weather satellites. From these last, you can hack weather pictures.

Satellites don't often use the HF (shortwave) spectrum because, in the case of objects circulating the earth, you want to be sure that the radio waves *won't* be reflected back by the ionosphere. Although satellites carrying worldwide television pictures use microwave frequencies (2 gigahertz and above), many satellites operate in the VHF and UHF portions of the radio frequency spectrum – 30 MHz to 1 GHz – and these present manageable problems in terms of reception. For a receiver you can either use a special-purpose machine which simply hears the radio traffic of interest and nothing else – it will probably be crystal-controlled – or a general purpose 'scanner' which allows you to type in the frequency of interest on a calculator-type keyboard. Such scanners pick up a huge variety of commercial, emergency, marine and aeronautical services. Cost is from £200 up, depending on the frequency range covered and additional facilities like memories and interfaces. Scanners can be purchased without licence, although in most countries their *use* is restricted. The more expensive scanners give you continuous coverage from about 25

MHz to over 1 GHz, but most of them have gaps, usually corresponding to areas used by the military or for conventional radio and television broadcasts. The frequencies you will need are:

amateur and educational	144-146 MHz
	430-440 MHz
weather satellites	136-138 MHz
	1690 MHz*
navigation satellites	159-151 MHz

*Most VHF/UHF scanners do not go as high as this and special down-converters are necessary.

Aerials suitable for these frequencies look like a horizontal-plane X in lightweight metal tubing. They are low-cost and obtainable by mail order out of amateur radio magazines. You need different sizes for different frequencies as they have to be 'tuned' for the service you are hunting for. More ambitious satellite hunters use steerable antennas. These look a little like TV aerials (the design is called Yagi) but they are controlled by rotators for both azimuth and elevation. Most of the satellites you look for are not geostationary; in other words, they do not stay in the same part of the sky with respect to a fixed earth location, so you have to track them. The simple antennas will receive signals from anything reasonably high in the sky, but at low signal strength; the more sophisticated steerable antennas are directional in design and, if correctly aimed, will bring in a far better signal.

On the amateur bands you will hear RTTY and ASCII transmissions of the sort already described. The educational satellites, Uosat 1 and Uosat 2, which are controlled from the University of Surrey, use a set of compressed protocols to relay data about the earth and its atmosphere. Details of both from AMSAT-UK, London E12 5EQ.

There are two sorts of weather satellite. The one that relays the pictures most familiar from television forecasts belongs to a family called Meteosat. Meteosats are geostationary and transmit, in the European area, at 1691.0 and 1694.5 MHz, which are in the low (S-band) microwave region. Reception equipment is expensive for the individual. The information comes down in a format called WEFAX and modules to decode it are available for both the BBC and IBM PC micros. Meteosats transmit global pictures, while the second type of weather satellite, called 'polar orbiting', transmit smaller portions of the world; they operate in the part of the radio spectrum between the civil VHF aircraft and commercial VHF, 136-137 MHz. US satellites can be heard at 137.5 and 137.62

MHz and Russian satellites are at 137.3, 137.4 and 137.62 MHz. There are a large number of other, non-weather, satellites in the same frequency band. The data format is called Automatic Picture Transmission (APT) and software packages to decode it and resolve pictures are available for a number of micros. Again, amateur radio magazines are a good source of advertisements.

10 Hacking: The Future

One reviewer of the first edition of this book suggested that the great days of hacking might already be over. This is palpable nonsense. Hacking already has a long history reaching back to the 1960s. Its antecedents in what I have called tech-freaking – lightly abusing technological artefacts to see what happens – go back even further. There is no reason to think that the intellectual curiosity which prompts people to undertake such activity has suddenly been snuffed out.

However, hacking has had a great deal of publicity lately. It has caught the fancy, not only of participants but of the general public as well. Quite simply, there has been rather a demand for spectacular hacking feats. But hacking doesn't happen to order. The big stories which have surfaced have two common features: there has always been a bright individual – or group of them – who liked the power of playing with big machines and making them misbehave in a controlled fashion; and there have been the opportunities offered by errors in security and design. The opportunities continue to come up, but not just because hackers want them to. So, viewed at any one time, the golden age of hacking always seems to have been yesterday ... until someone stumbles across a fresh opportunity.

What certainly has happened is that hackers are much less communicative and far less likely to shout their triumphs to the nearest journalist. There are two reasons for this: first, the authorities in both the UK and the USA are showing a greater tendency to attempt prosecution. These prosecutions are not always successful and are often born of the need to be 'doing something' about computer crime – chasing amateur hackers is much easier than tracking down professional computer fraudsters. The second reason is that hackers are beginning to realize that one of the areas where they can occasion real harm is in publicizing their feats. So the signs are that, for the moment, there will be less about hacking in the press for the next few years. It will be going on though; the challenges continue to beckon.

During the last year we have had a number of hacking hoaxes aimed at the gullibility of would-be hackers and, more importantly, at journalists. It is now quite easy to make a micro look like a 'sensitive' mainframe. To show how it is done, I will describe a stunt I had planned for 1 April 1985 but which, for reasons I will explain, I did not switch on.

I decided to give my fellow enthusiasts a treat: the opportunity to enter what they would think was the UK's ultimate target, a computer resource of MI5, the security service. It required two elements, a database 'host' and a plausible environment. For the first I selected a well-known bulletin-board package and reconfigured it. I didn't want the messaging, I did require the sign-on and password validation facilities, the menu generators and facilities to display files and, in the case of this particular package, the ability to call extra programs while the user remained under the control of the bulletin-board package. My victims weren't going to realize it, but all they would be actually be seeing were a series of text files. The whole thing was designed a little like an adventure game with a series of 'rooms' Now to make it plausible. In recent years investigative journalists have written in some detail about the internal organization of MI5 – the names of the departments and their functions. A good deal came out during the aftermath of the trial of Michael Bettaney. So raw material was not difficult to come by. The success of the hoax, I decided, would depend on making my victims think they were making discoveries, rather than laying it all out in an obvious fashion. In this way they would participate in their own downfall. The sign-on page made no interesting announcements; it merely asked: 'Password?'. Actually it accepted a whole list of hacker's favourites: 'TEST', 'DEMO', that kind of thing. Once admitted, the opening menu stated:

```
2900 SERIES REMOTE TEST FACILITY
All log-ons to be reported on Form T/V002/658/81 to Room
3002 within 3 working hours
Facility permits test of gateway interconnects only
```

There were no further instructions, but if you typed 'HELP', you got the following:

```
Facility connects and tests all Gateways available via S1
and S2 and provides, where appropriate, dummy account
databases for response testing
```

If you typed 'GATEWAY' you were provided with a list of interesting-sounding remote computers: PNC (Police National Computer), DHSS facilities, etc., as well as minicomputers corresponding to known MI5 sections. There were also links to

'Century' (you had to guess that was MI6, the headquarters of which is called Century House) and to Cheltenham, and so on. I also gave 'MI5' an electronic mail service, presumably for field agents. If you tried to test out these gateways, you would usually get several screenfuls of carriage returns, some random characters and then a message like:

```
Gateway linking in....please wait
```

or

```
Gateway facilities not available under this ID
```

For even more intrepid explorers I could offer further menus, which would gradually prompt him or her to the conclusion that this was indeed a mega-target. As soon as my imagination gave way at any point I had an easy way of disposing of my victims: I could either dump them in a message stating: 'INAPROPRIATE AUTHORIZATION' or, more fun this, 'UNAUTHORIZED ACCESS, USER ID REVOKED, PLEASE CONTACT SUPERVISOR CSH RM 2003 IMMEDIATELY' ('CSH' stood for Curzon Street House, headquarters building of MI5), or I could simply log them off without explanation.

The scenario was that the victim had stumbled on a computer port which allowed a sensitive network to be tested. Incidentally, most networks do have such facilities. I never carried out the hoax because, shortly before I was to initiate my victims by leaving tantalizing 'Try this funny number' messages on hackers' bulletin boards, MI5 went into another of its high-profile phases. A discontented member of its staff, Cathy Massitter, decided to tell a TV program that she thought MI5 were concentrating too much on targets that presented little threat to national security even if their aims were politically unpopular. It was the first time such an interview had been given and it was obvious that a further MI5 scandal – my hoax had a fair chance of reaching the newspapers – would cause much more reaction than I had originally bargained for. By the time the Massitter affair had disappeared from the front pages hacking itself was in the news – Hugo Cornwall was suddenly notorious, and two people had been arrested on alleged hacking charges. So the MI5 caper never happened. But now I treat each new hacking story with considerable scepticism until I can test it out with my own general knowledge of how computers and networks actually operate.

I am not certain how many more hacking prosecutions we will see; some victims certainly want to fight back, but the results from going to law are uncertain. As we saw right at the beginning, hacking itself is not a crime and the would-be prosecutor must find a crime to fit the particular circumstances of an event. However, each time the accused come before the courts, the message that comes across is not 'Hacking doesn't pay' but 'X have an insecure computer – amateurs could break into it.' If the prosecution is unsuccessful, Company X has not only a hacking problem, it has a Public Relations Disaster.

Security is now probably the biggest single growth area within the mainstream computer business. At conference after conference, consultants compete with each other to produce the most frightening statistics.

The main concern, however, is not hacking but fraud. Donn Parker, a frequent writer and speaker on computer crime based at the Stanford Research Institute, has put US computer fraud at $3000 million a year, although reported crimes amount to only $100 million annually. In June 1983 the *Daily Telegraph* claimed that British computer-related frauds could be anything between £500 million and £2.5 billion a year. Detective Inspector Ken McPherson, former head of the computer crime unit of the Metropolitan Police, was quoted in 1983 as saying that within fifteen years every fraud would involve a computer. The trouble is, very few victims are prepared to acknowledge their losses. To date, no British clearing bank has admitted to suffering from an out-and-out computer fraud, other than the doctoring of credit and plastic ID cards. Few consultants believe that they have been immune.

However, to put the various threats in perspective, here are two recent US assessments. Robert P. Campbell of Advanced Information Management, formerly head of computer security in the US Army, reckons that only one computer crime in 100 is detected; of those detected, 15 per cent or fewer are reported to the authorities; and of those reported, one in thirty three is successfully prosecuted – a 'success' rate of one in 22,000.

Robert Courtney, former security chief at IBM, produced a list of hazards to computers: 'The No. 1 problem now and forever is errors and omissions.' Then there is crime by insiders, particularly nontechnical people of three types: single women under thirty-five; 'little old ladies' over fifty who want to give the money to charity; and older men who feel their careers have left them neglected. Next, natural disasters. Sabotage by disgruntled employees. Water damage. As for hackers and other outsiders who break in, he estimates it is less than 3 per cent of the total.

Here in the UK the National Computing Centre says that at least 90 per cent of computer crimes involve putting false information into a computer, as opposed to sophisticated logic techniques; such crimes are identical to conventional embezzlement – looking for weaknesses in an accounting system and taking advantage. In such cases the computer merely carries out the fraud with more thoroughness than a human and the printout gives the accounts a spurious air of being correct. The *Computer Fraud Survey*, published in 1985 by the Audit Commission, came to similar conclusions. It received 943 replies to its general-purpose survey and found seventy-seven instances of fraud. Fifty-eight of these were frauds committed at inputting stage, two at the output stage and seventeen involved misuse of resources by company employees. There was no instance of penetration by an outsider.

Elsewhere, a thriving trade is developing in the publication of newsletters about computer security. Newsletters, typically costing in excess of £200 p.a., are a way of making businessmen pay even more for their information. They usually consist of eight or twelve typewritten pages and promise exclusive news fast to the decision-making executive. In the last few months of 1985 no less than three new computer security newsletters have emerged to challenge the well-established *Computer Fraud & Security Bulletin* – and they have all lead off with 'exclusive' analyses of the hacking threat. Without exception, they have been appallingly bad, relying on newspaper clippings from the popular press, a notoriously sloppy source of information, and even getting readily checkable incidents and dates completely wrong.

In the meantime we are on the threshold of a new age of opportunities for the hacker: the technology we can afford has suddenly become much more interesting.

The most recent new free magazines to which I continue to acquire subscriptions are for owners of the IBM PC, its variants and clones. There are several UK monthlies for regular users, another for corporate buyers, a weekly, and several US titles. The IBM PC is only partly aimed at small-business users as a stand-alone machine to run accounting, wordprocessing, spreadsheet calculation and the usual business dross; increasingly the marketing is pitching it as an executive workstation so that the corporate employee can not only carry out functions local to his own office but access the corporate mainframe as well – for data, messaging with colleagues, and for greater processing power.

In page after page the articles debate the future of this development – do employees *want* workstations, don't many bosses still feel that anything to do with typing is best left to their secretary? How does the executive workstation relate to the mainframe? Do you allow the executive merely to *collect* data from it or to input as well? If you permit the latter, what effect will this have on the integrity of the mainframe's files? How do you control what is going on? What is the future of the DP professional? Who is in charge?

And so the articles go on. Is IBM about to offer packages which integrate mainframes and PCs in one enormous system, thus effectively blocking out every other computer manufacturer and software publisher in the world by sheer weight and presence?

I don't know the answers to these questions but elsewhere in these same magazines is evidence that the hardware products to support the executive workstation revolution are there – the leading contender is the IRMA range of cards. The products are high-quality terminal emulators; not the sort of thing hitherto achieved in software – variants on asynchronous protocols with some fancy cursor addressing – but cards capable of supporting a variety of key synchronous communications like 327x (bisynch and SDLC) and handling high-speed file transfers in CICs, TSO, IMS and CMS. These products feature special facilities like windowing or replicate aspects of mainframe operating systems like VM (Virtual Machine) giving the user the experience of having several different computers simultaneously at his or her command. Other cards can handle IBM's smaller mini-mainframes, the Systems/34 and /38. Nor are other mainframe manufacturers with oddball comms requirements ignored: ICL, Honeywell and Burroughs are all catered for. You can turn a PC into a Unix-like machine. There are even several PC add-ons which give it direct X.25; it can sit on a packet-switched network without the aid of a PAD.

Such products are perhaps expensive by personal micro standards but it means that, for the expenditure of around £5000, the hacker can call up formidable power from his machine. The addition of special environments on these new super micros which give the owner direct experience of mainframe operating systems – and the manuals to go with them – will greatly increase the population of knowledgeable computer buffs. Add to this the fact that the corporate workstation market, if it is at all successful, must mean that many executives will want to call their mainframe from home – there will be many many more computer ports on the PTSN or sitting on PSS.

More and more networks, public and private, are being opened up. If there is one thing which distinguishes the British hacker from his US cousin it is that the latter have had more opportunity to explore data networks. But now there is increasing demand to provide links and gateways between various services, and to supply smooth user interfaces. These are all wonderful opportunities.

There can be little doubt that the need for system security will play an increasing role in the specification of new mainframe installations. For some time hardware and software engineers have known the technical devices necessary to make a computer secure; the difficulty is to get regular users to implement the appropriate methods – humans can only memorize a limited number of passwords. I expect greater use will be made of threat-monitoring techniques – checking for sequences of unsuccessful attempts at logging in, monitoring the level of usage of customers for extent, timing, and which terminals or ports they appear on. The drawback of threat-monitoring programs is that they demand a large chunk of the computer's overhead, so that the services they are supposed to be protecting run more slowly, thus hindering legitimate users. There is now a substantial trade in system add-ons to increase security – encryption boxes, dial-back modems and the like. Please, I don't want any more invitations from manufacturers to PR functions launching such products. They do not necessarily make life more difficult for the hacker. Computer security is a matter of looking at the entire system and the environment in which it is used, not just adding black boxes. I *know* such boxes, if attacked directly, would defeat me. I would be looking for those areas in the overall system which the presence of the black box had made *more* vulnerable – because everyone now had a false sense that the security problem was over.

So far as hackers are concerned, it is the difficulty of the exercise that motivates us rather than the prospect of instant wealth. It is also the flavour of naughty, but not outright, illegality. I remember how the Citizens' Band radio boom of a few years ago started quietly with just a handful of London breakers who had imported US sets, really simply to talk to a few friends. One day everyone woke up, switched on their rigs and discovered overnight there was a whole new subculture out there, breathing the ether. Every day there were more and more until no spare channels could be found. Then some talented engineers found out how to freak the rigs and add another forty channels to the original forty. And then another forty. Suddenly there were wholesalers and retailers and fanzines, all selling and promoting products the very importing or manufacturing of which was illegal under British law.

Finally the government introduced a legalized CB, using different standards from the imported US ones. Within six months the illegal scene had contracted violently and no legal CB service of comparable size ever took its place. Manufacturers and shopkeepers who had expected to make a financial killing were left with warehouses full of the stuff. Much of the attraction of AM CB was that it was forbidden and unregulated. There is the desire to be an outlaw, but clever and not too outrageous with it, in very many of us.

So I don't believe that hacking can be stopped by tougher security or by legislation or even by the fear of punishment. Don't get me wrong; I regard computers as vastly beneficial to humankind, but they can threaten our traditional concepts of freedom, individuality and human worth. I like to believe hacking at its best provides a path to a curious reassertion of some of those ideas.

The challenge of hacking is deeply engrained in many computer enthusiasts; where else can you find an activity the horizons of which are constantly expanding, where new challenges and dangers can be found every day, where you are not playing a visibly artificial 'game', where so much can be accessed with so few resources as a small keyboard, a glowing VDU, an inquisitive and acquisitive brain, and an impish mentality?

Appendix I
Trouble Shooting

The assumption is that you are operating in the default mode of 300/300 bits/s asynchronous, using CCITT tones, 7 bits, even parity, one stop bit, full duplex/echo off, originate. You have dialled the remote number, seized the line and can hear a data tone. Something is not working properly. This is a partial list of possibilities.

The screen remains blank
A physical link has failed. Check the cables between computer, modem and phone line.
The remote modem needs waking up. Send a ‹cr› or failing that, an ENQ (‹ctrl›E) character.
The remote modem is operating at a different speed. Some modems can be brought up to speed by hitting successive ‹cr›s; they usually begin at 110 bits/s and then go to 300, so two successive ‹cr›s should do the trick.
The remote modem is not working at V.21 standards, either because it is a different CCITT standard, e.g. V.22, V.22 bis, V.23 etc., or operates on Bell (US) tones. Since different standards tend to have different 'wake-up' tones which are easily recognized with practice, you may be able to spot what is happening. It shouldn't need to be said that if you are calling a North American service you should assume Bell tones.
Both your modem and that of the remote service are in answer or in originate and so cannot 'speak' to each other. Always assume you are in the originate mode.
The remote service is not using ASCII/International Alphabet No. 5.

The screen fills with random characters
Data format different from your defaults. Check 7- or 8-bit characters, even/odd parity, stop and start bits.
Mismatch of characters owing to misdefined protocol. Check start/stop, try alternately EOB/ACK and XON/XOF.
Remote computer operating at a different speed from you. Try, in order, 110, 300, 600, 1200, 75.

Poor physical connection. If using an acoustic coupler check location of handset; if not, listen on line to see if it is noisy or crossed.

The remote service is not using ASCII/International Alphabet No. 5.

Every character appears twice
You are actually in half-duplex mode and the remote computer as well as your own are both sending characters to your screen. Switch to full duplex/echo off.

All information appears on only one line, which is constantly overwritten
The remote service is not sending carriage returns. If your terminal software has the facility, enable it to induce carriage returns when each display line is filled. Many on-line services and public dial-up ports let you configure the remote port to send carriage returns and vary line length. Your software may have a facility to show control characters, in which case you will see ‹ctrl›J if the remote service is sending carriage returns.

Wide spaces appear between display lines
The remote service is sending carriage returns and your software is inducing another one simultaneously. Turn off your induced carriage-return facility. In 'show control character' mode, you will see ‹ctrl›Js.

Display lines are broken awkwardly
The remote service is expecting your screen to support more characters than it is able. Professional services tend to expect eighty characters across whilst many personal computers may have less than forty, so that they can be read on a TV screen. Check if your software can help, but you may have to live with it. Alternatively, the remote computer may let you reconfigure its character stream.

Most of the display makes sense, but every so often it becomes garbled
You have intermittent line noise. Check if you can command the remote computer to send the same stream again and see if you get the garbling.

The remote service is sending graphics instructions which your computer and software can't resolve.

The display contains recognizable characters in definite groupings, but otherwise makes no sense
The data is intended for an intelligent terminal which will combine the transmitted data with a local program so that it makes sense.
The data is intended for batch processing.
The data is encrypted.

Although the stream of data appears properly on my VDU, when I try to print it out, I get corruption and overprinting
Most printers use a series of special control characters to enable various functions – line feeds, backspace, double intensity, special graphics, etc. The remote service is sending a series of control characters which, although not displayed on your screen, are 'recognized' by your printer, although often in not very helpful ways. You may be able to correct the worst problems in software, by for example, enabling line feeds; alternatively many printers can be reconfigured in hardware by appropriate settings of DIL switches internally.

When accessing a videotex service, the screen fills with squares
The square is the standard display default if your videotex terminal can't make sense of the data being sent to it. There could be several reasons.

Check physical connections and listen for line noise.

The videotex host does not work to UK videotex standards. French videotex uses parallel attributes and has a number of extra features. The CEPT standard for Europe contains features from both the UK and French systems and you may be able to recognize some of the display. North American videotex is alphageometric and sends line-drawing instructions rather than characters.

The videotex host has enhanced graphics features, perhaps for dynamically redefined character sets, alphageometric instructions, or alphaphotographic (full resolution) pictures. If the host has some UK standard-compatible features, you will be able to read them normally. If the cursor jumps about the screen, the host has dynamic graphics facilities. If the videotex protocol is anything at all like the UK standard, you should see regular clear-screens as each new page comes up; however, advanced graphics features tend to work by suppressing clear-screens.

The service you have dialled is not using videotex. PSS is accessible at 75/1200, as are one or two direct-dial services. In this case you should be seeing a conventional display or trying one of the other suggestions in this appendix. It is usual to assume that any subscriber dialling into a 75/1200 port has only a forty-character display.

I can't see what I am typing
The remote computer is not echoing back to you. Switch to half-duplex. If the remote computer's messages now appear doubled, that is unusual but not unique. You will have to toggle back to full duplex for receive.

Data seems to come from the remote computer in jerky bursts rather than as a smooth stream
If you are using PSS or a similar packet-switched service and it is near peak business hours either in your time zone or in that of the host you are accessing, the effect is due to heavy packet traffic. There is nothing you can do. Do not send extra commands to 'speed things up' as those commands will eventually arrive at the host and cause unexpected results.
The host is pausing for a EOB/ACK or XON/XOF message. Check your protocol settings; try sending ‹ctrl›Q or ‹ctrl›F.

I have an apparently valid password but it is not accepted
You don't have a valid password or you don't have all of it.
The password has hidden control characters which don't display on the screen. Watch out for ‹ctrl›H – the backspace – which will overwrite an existing displayed character.
The password contains characters which your computer doesn't normally generate. Check your terminal software and see if there is a way of sending them.

Most of the time everything works smoothly, but I can't get past certain prompts
The remote service is looking for characters your computer doesn't normally generate. Check your terminal software and see if there is a way of sending them.

A list or file called up turns out to be boring – can I stop it?
Try sending ‹ctrl›S; this may simply make the remote machine pause until a ‹ctrl›Q is sent, and you may find the list resumes where it left off. On the other hand, it may take you onto a menu.
2 Send a BREAK signal (‹ctrl›1). If one BREAK doesn't work, send another in quick succession.

I wish to get into the operating system from an applications program

Don't we all? There is no standard way of doing this and indeed it might be almost impossible because the operating system can only be addressed by a few privileged terminals, of which yours (and its associated password) is not one. However, you could try the following:

Immediately after signing on, send two BREAKs (‹ctrl›1).

Immediately after signing on, try combinations of ‹esc›, ‹ctrl› and ‹shift›. As a desperate measure, send two carriage returns before signing on – this has been known to work!

At an options page, try requesting SYSTEM or some obvious contraction like SYS or X. If in the Basic language, depending on the dialect, SYSTEM or X in immediate mode should get you the operating system.

I am trying to capture data traffic from a short-wave radio and am having little success

Your computer could be emitting so much radio noise itself that any signal you are attempting to hear is squashed. To test, tune your radio to a fairly quiet short-wave broadcast and then experiment listening to the background hash with the computer switched first on, then off. If the noise level drops when you turn off the computer, then you need to arrange for more RF suppression and to move the computer and radio farther apart. Another source of RF noise is the sync scan in a TV tube.

If you can hear the two tones of RTTY traffic but can't get letters resolved, check that your terminal unit is locking onto the signal (often indicated by LEDs). You should then at least get some response on your screen, if it doesn't make immediate sense.

Once you have letters on screen, try altering the speed at which you are receiving (see chapter 9); check also that you are reading in the right 'sense', i.e. that 'mark' and 'space' have not been reversed.

In addition to signals sent with the conventional International Telegraphic Code No. 2 (Baudot), variants exist for foreign letter sets, like Cyrillic, which your software may not be able to resolve.

There are other data-type services which sound a little like RTTY, but are not: they include FAX (facsimile), Hellschreiber (a form of remote dot-matrix printing), SITOR (see chapter 9) and special military/diplomatic systems like piccolo.

Appendix II Eclectic Glossary

This glossary collects together the sort of name, word, abbreviation or phrase you could come across during your network adventures and for which you may not be able to find a precise meaning.

ACK Non-printing character used in some comms protocols to indicate that a block has been received and that more can be sent; used in association with EOB.

ANSI American National Standards Institute, one of a number of standards organizations.

Answer mode When a modem is set up to receive calls, the usual mode for a host. The user's computer will be in originate.

ARQ Automatic repeat request, a method of error correction.

ASCII American Standard Code for Information Interchange, alternative name for International Telegraphic Alphabet No. 5, a 7-bit code to symbolize common characters and comms instructions, usually transmitted as 8-bit code to include a parity bit.

ASR Automatic send receive – any keyboard terminal capable of generating a message into off-line storage for later transmission; includes paper-tape telex machines as well as microcomputers.

Asynchronous Description of communications which rely on 'start' and 'stop' bits to synchronize originator and receiver of data – hence asynchronous protocols, channels, modems, terminals, etc.

Backward channel Supervisory channel, not used as main channel of communication; in viewdata the 75 baud back from the user to the host.

Baseband modulation This is direct on the comms line rather than using audio or radio frequencies. Used in some local area networks. A baseband or 'short-haul' modem can be used to link computers in adjacent offices, but not over telephone lines

Baud rate Measure of the signalling rate on a data channel, number of signalling elements per second; not the same as bits/s.

Baudot 5-bit data code used in telegraphy, telex and RTTY; also known as International Telegraph Alphabet No. 2.

Bell (*1*) BEL, non-printing character which sounds a bell or bleep, usually enabled by ‹ctrl›G. (*2*) Common name for US phone company and, in this context, specifiers for a number of data standards and services, e.g. Bell 103a, 202a, 212a, etc. See appendix V.

Bisynchronous IBM protocol involving synchronous transmission of binary coded data.

Bit Binary digit – value 0 or 1.

Bits/s Bits per second: the rate at which information is passed along a data channel. Not the same as baud rate (*q.v.*).

BLAISE British Library Automated Information Service, a substantial bibliographic on-line host.

BREAK Non-printing character used in some data transmission protocols and found on some terminals. Can sometimes be regenerated by using ‹ctrl›1.

Broadband Broadband data channels have a wider bandwidth than ordinary telephone circuits – twelve times in fact – to give a bandwidth of 48 kHz, over which many simultaneous high-speed data transfers can take place.

Broadcast service Data service in which all users receive the same information simultaneously, without the opportunity to interrogate or query; e.g. news services like AP, Reuters News, UPI etc. Compare on-line services.

BSC Binary synchronous communications; see bisynchronous.

Byte Group of bits (8) representing one data character.

Call accept In packet switching, the packet which confirms the party is willing to proceed with the call.

Call redirection In packet switching, allows call to be automatically redirected from original address to another, nominated, address.

Call request In packet switching, packet sent to initiate a data call.

CCITT Comité Consultatif International Téléphonique et Télégraphique – committee of International Telecommunications Union – which sets international comms standards. Only the USA fails to follow its recommendations in terms of modem tones, preferring 'Bell (*q.v.*) tones'. The CCITT also sets such standards as V.21, V.24, X.25 etc.

Character terminal In packet switching, a terminal which can only access via a PAD.

Cluster When two or more terminals are connected to a data channel at a single point.

Common carrier A telecommunications resource providing facilities to the public.

Connect time Length of time connected to a remote computer, often the measure of payment, contrast with CPU time (*q.v.*) or CPU units, which measures how much 'effort' the host put into the communication.

CPS Characters per second.

CPU time In an on-line session, the amount of time the central processor actually spends on the interaction process, as opposed to connect time; either can be used as the basis of tariffing.

CRC Cyclic redundancy check, an error-detection method.

CUG Closed user group, a group of users/terminals who enjoy privacy with respect to a public service.

Datacall In packet switching, an ordinary call, sometimes called a 'switched virtual call'.

Dataline In packet switching, dedicated line between customer's terminal and packet-switch exchange (PSE).

DCE Data circuit-terminating equipment; officialese for modems.

DES Data Encryption Standard, a US-approved method of encrypting data traffic, and somewhat controversial in its effectiveness.

Dialog Well-established on-line host available worldwide covering an extensive range of scientific, bibliographic and news services. Also known as Lockheed Dialog.

Dial-up Call initiated via PTSN, no matter where it goes after that, as opposed to service available via permanent leased line.

DTE Data terminal equipment; officialese for computers.

Datel BT's name for its data services, covering both the equipment and the type of line, for example, Datel 100 corresponds to telegraph circuits, Datel 200 is the usual 300/300 asynchronous service, Datel 400 is for one-way transmissions, such as monitoring of remote sites, Datel 600 is a two- or four-wire asynchronous service at up to 1200 baud, Datel 2400 typically uses a four-wire private circuit at 2400 baud synchronous, etc.

Duplex Transmission in two directions simultaneously, sometimes called full duplex; contrast half duplex, in which alternate transmissions by either end are required. (N.B. This is terminology used in data communications over land lines. Just to confuse matters radio technology refers to simplex, when only one party can transmit at a time and a single radio frequency is used, two-frequency simplex or half-duplex when only one party can speak but two frequencies are used, as in repeater and remote base working; and full duplex when both parties can speak simultaneously and two radio frequencies are used, as in radio telephones.)

EBCDIC Extended Binary Coded Decimal Interchange Code – IBM's alternative to ASCII, based on an 8-bit code, usually transmitted synchronously. 256 characters are available.

Echo (*1*) When a remote computer sends back to the terminal each letter as it receives it for confirming redisplay locally. (*2*) Effect on long comms lines caused by successive amplifications. Echo suppressors are introduced to prevent disturbance caused by this phenomenon, but in some data transmission the echo suppressors must be switched off.

EIA Electronic Industries Association, US standards body.

80-80 Type of circuit used for telex and telegraphy; mark and space are indicated by conditions of − or + 80 volts. Also known in the UK as Tariff J. The usual telex speed is 50 baud, private wire telegraphy (news agencies, etc.) 75 baud.

Emulator Software/hardware set-up which makes one device mimic another; for example, a personal computer may emulate an industry-standard intelligent terminal like the VT100. Compare simulator, which gives one device the attributes of another, but not necessarily in real time, for example, when a large mini carries a program making it simulate another computer to develop software.

ENQ Non-printing character signifying 'who are you?' and often sent by hosts as they are dialled up. When the user's terminal receives ENQ it may be programmed to send out a password automatically. Corresponds to ‹esc›E.

EOB End of block, non-printing character used in some protocols, usually in association with ACK.

EPAD Variant on PSS PAD which gives error correction

facilities between PAD and user's (character) terminal; see chapter 7.

Equalization Method of compensation for distortion over long comms channels.

Euronet-Diane European direct-access information network.

FDM Frequency division multiplexing, a wide-bandwidth transmission medium, e.g. coaxial cable, which supports several narrow-bandwidth channels by differentiating by frequency. Compare time division multiplexing.

FSK Frequency shift keying, a simple signalling method in which frequencies but not phase or amplitude are varied according to whether '1' or '0' is sent. Used in low-speed asynchronous comms both over land line and by radio.

Handshaking Hardware and software rules for remote devices to communicate with each other which include supervisory signals such as 'wait' 'acknowledge', 'transmit', 'ready to receive', etc.

Hayes protocols Set of *de facto* standard commands for intelligent modems often used by software packages.

HDLC In packet switching, high-level data-link control procedure, an international standard which detects and corrects errors in the stream of data between the terminal and the exchange and to provides flow control.

Host The 'big' computer holding the information the user wishes to retrieve.

Infoline Scientific on-line service from Pergamon.

ISB See sideband.

ISO International Standards Organization.

Kermit Error-correction protocol widely installed on a large number of mainframes, minis and micros.

KSR Keyboard send receive, terminal with keyboard on which anything that is typed is immediately sent, no off-line preparation facility, e.g. teletypewriter, and 'dumb' terminals.

LAN Local area network; normally using coaxial cable, this form of network operates at high speed over an office or works site, but no farther. It may have an interconnect facility to PTSN or **PSS**.

LF Line feed, the cursor moves active position down one line. The usual code is ‹ctrl›J. It is not the same as carriage return which merely sends the cursor to left-hand side of the line it already occupies. However, in many protocols/terminals/set-ups, hitting the ‹ret› or ‹enter› button means both ‹lf› and ‹cr›.

Logical channel Apparently continuous path from one terminal to another.

LSB See sideband.

Macro Software facility frequently found in comms programs which permits the preparation and sending of commonly used strings of information, particularly passwords and routing instructions.

Mark One of the two conditions on a data communications line, the other being 'space'; mark indicates idle and is used as a stop bit.

Message switching When a complete message is stored and then forwarded, as opposed to a packet of information. This technique is used in some electronic mail services, but not for general data transmission.

Modem Modulator–demodulator.

Multiplexer Device which divides a data channel into two or more independent channels.

MultiStream BT variant on PSS to make it more user-friendly; includes EPAD and VPAD (*q.v.*).

MVS Multiple virtual storage, an IBM operating system dating from the mid-seventies.

NUA Network user address, the number by which each terminal on a packet-switch network is identified (character terminals don't have them individually, because they use a PAD). In PSS it is a twelve-digit number.

NUI Network user identity, used in PSS for dial-up access by each user.

Octet In packet switching, 8 consecutive bits of user data, e.g. one character.

On-line service Interrogative or query service available for dial-up. Examples include Lockheed Dialog, Blaise, Dow Jones News Retrieval, etc.; leased-line examples include Reuters Monitor and Telerate.

Originate mode Setting for a modem operated by a user about to call another computer.

OSI Open Systems Interconnect, intended world standard for digital network connections. Compare SNA.

Packet switching See chapter 7.

Packet terminal Terminal capable of creating and disassembling packets, interacting with a packet network. Compare character terminal.

PAD Packet assembly/disassembly device, which permits 'ordinary' terminals to connect to packet-switch services by providing addressing headers (and removal), protocol conversion, etc.

Parity checking Technique of error correction in which one bit is added to each data character so that the number of bits is always even (or always odd).

PDP 8 & 11 Large family of minis, commercially very successful, made by DEC. the PDP 8 was 12-bit, the PDP 11 is 16-bit. The LSI 11 have strong family connections to the PDP 11, as have some configurations of the desktop Rainbow.

Polling Method of controlling terminals on a clustered data network where each is called in turn by the computer to see if it wishes to transmit or receive.

Protocol Agreed set of rules.

PSE Packet-switch exchange, which enables packet-switching in a network.

PTSN Public switched telephone network, the voice-grade telephone network dialled from a phone, in contrast with leased lines, digital networks, conditioned lines, etc.

PTT Common term for the publicly owned telecommunications authority/utility in various countries.

PVC Permanent virtual circuit, a connection in packet switching which is always open; no set-up is required.

Redundancy checking Method of error correction.

RS232C EIA RS232C is the list of definitions for interchange circuit; the US term for CCITT V.24. See appendix III.

RSX-11 Popular operating system for PDP 11 family.

RTTY Radio teletype – method of sending telegraphy over radio waves.

RUBOUT Back-space deleting character, using ‹ctrl›H.

Secondary channel Data channel, usually used for supervision, using same physical path as main channel. In V.23 which is usually 600 or 1200 baud half-duplex, 75-baud traffic is supervisory, but in viewdata it is the channel back from the user to the host, thus giving low-cost full duplex.

Segment Chargeable unit of volume on PSS.

Serial Transmission 1 bit at a time, using a single pair of wires, as opposed to parallel transmission, in which several bits are sent simultaneously over a ribbon cable. A serial interface often uses many more than two wires between computer and modem or computer and printer, but only two wires carry the data traffic, the remainder being used for supervision, electrical power and earthing, or not at all.

Sideband In radio the technique of suppressing the main carrier and limiting the transmission to the information-bearing sideband. To listen at the receiver, the carrier is re-created locally. The technique, which produces large economies in channel occupancy, is extensively used in professional, non-broadcast applications. The full name is single sideband, suppressed carrier. Each full carrier supports two sidebands, an upper and a lower, (USB and LSB respectively); in general, USB is used for speech, LSB for data, but this is only a convention – amateurs use LSB for speech below 10 MHz, for example. ISB, independent sideband, is when the one carrier supports two sidebands with separate information on them, usually speech on one and data on the other. If you listen to radio teletype on the 'wrong' sideband, 'mark' and 'space' values become reversed with a consequent loss of meaning.

SITOR Error-correction protocol for sending data over a radio path using frequent checks and acknowledgements. Used in the maritime service. The amateur equivalent is called AMTOR.

SNA System Network Architecture, IBM proprietary networking protocol, the rival to OSI.

Space One of two binary conditions in a data transmission channel, the other being 'mark'. Space is binary 0.

Spooling Simultaneous peripheral operation on-line. More usually, the ability, while accessing a database, to store all fetched information in a local memory buffer, from which it may be recalled for later examination or dumped to disk or printer.

Start/Stop Asynchronous transmission; the 'start' and 'stop' bits bracket each data character.

Statistical multiplexer A statmux is an advanced multiplexer which divides one physical link between several data channels, taking advantage of the fact that not all channels bear equal traffic loads.

STX Start text, non-printing character used in some protocols.

SVC Switched virtual circuit; in packet switching, when connection between two computers or computer and terminal must be set up by a specific call.

SYN Non-printing character often used in synchronous transmission to tell a remote device to start its local timing mechanism.

Synchronous Data transmission in which timing information is superimposed on pure data. Under this method, 'start/stop' techniques are not used and data exchange is more efficient, hence synchronous channel, modem, terminal, protocol, etc.

TDM Time division multiplexer, a technique for sharing several data channels along one high-grade physical link. It is not as efficient as statistical techniques.

Telenet US packet-switch common carrier.

Teletex High-speed replacement for telex, 2400 baud, as yet to find much commercial support.

Teletext Use of vertical blanking interval in broadcast television to transmit magazines of text information, for example BBC's Ceefax and IBA's Oracle.

Telex Public switched low-speed telegraph network.

Tempest Set of standards to reduce the opportunities for electronmagnetic eavesdropping on VDUs, printers, etc. See chapter 6.

3101 IBM intelligent display terminal emulation sometimes included on asynchronous comms packages; it has limited windowing capacity.

3270 IBM interactive bisynchronous terminal usually sitting direct on mainframes or connected via cluster controllers.

TOPIC The Stock Exchange's market price display service; it comes down a leased line and has some of the qualities of both viewdata and teletext.

TOPS Operating system found on DEC mainframes like the DEC-10 and -20.

Tymnet US packet-switch common carrier.

V standards Set of recommendations by CCITT. See appendix III.

VAX Super-mini family made by DEC; often uses VMS or Unix operating systems.

Videotex Technology allowing a large number of users to access data easily on terminal based (originally) on modified TV sets. Information is presented in 'page' format rather than on a scrolling screen and the user issues all commands on a numbers-only keypad. Various standards exist of which the UK one is so far dominant; other include the European CEPT standard which is similar to the UK one, a French version and the US Presentation Level Protocol. Transmission speeds are usually 1200 baud from the host and 75 baud from the user. Previously referred to in the UK as viewdata.

Virtual In the present context, a virtual drive, store, machine etc., is one which appears to the user to exist, but is merely an illusion generated on a computer; thus several users of IBM's VM operating system each think they have an entire separate computer, complete with drives, disks and other peripherals. In fact, the one actual machine can support several lower-level operating systems simultaneously.

VPAD Variant on PSS PAD which allows videotex terminals to operate with full support – part of BT's MultiStream.

VT52/100 Industry-standard general purpose computer terminals with no storage capacity or processing power but with the ability to be locally programmed to accept a variety of asynchronous transmission protocols. Manufactured by DEC. The series has developed since the VT100.

X standards Set of recommendations by CCITT. See appendix III.

XON/XOF Pair of non-printing characters sometimes used in protocols to tell devices when to start or stop sending. XON often corresponds to ‹ctrl›Q and XOF to ‹ctrl›S.

Appendix III Selected CCITT Recommendations

V series: Data Transmission over Telephone Circuits

V.1	Power levels for data transmission over telephone lines
V.3	International Alphabet No. 5 (ASCII)
V.4	General structure of signals of IA5 code for data transmission over public telephone network
V.5	Standardization of modulation rates and data signalling rates for synchronous transmission in general switched network
V.6	Ditto, on leased circuits
V.13	Answerback simulator
V.15	Use of acoustic coupling for data transmission
V.19	Modems for parallel data transmission using telephone signalling frequencies
V.20	Parallel data transmission modems standardized for universal use in the general switched telephone network
V.21	200 bits/s modem standardized
V.22	1200 bits/s full-duplex two-wire modem for PTSN
V.22 bis	2400 bits/s full-duplex two-wire modem for PTSN
V.23	600/1200 bits/s modem for PTSN
V.24	List of definitions for interchange circuits between data terminal equipment and data circuit-terminating equipment
V.25	Automatic calling and/or answering equipment on PTSN
V.26	2400 bits/s modem on 4-wire circuit
V.26 bis	2400/1200 bits/s modem for PTSN
V.27	4800 bits/s modem for leased circuits
V.27 bis	4800 bits/s modem (equalised) for leased circuits
V.27 ter	4800 bits/s modem for PTSN
V.29	9600 bits/s modem for leased circuits
V.35	Data transmission at 48 kbits/s using 60-108 kHz band circuits

X series: Recommendations Covering Data Networks

X.1	International user classes of services in public data networks
X.2	International user facilities in public data networks
X.3	Packet assembly/disassembly facility (PAD)
X.4	General structure of signals of IA5 code for transmission over public data networks
X.20	Interface between data terminal equipment and data circuit-terminating equipment for start/stop transmission services on public data networks
X.20 bis	V.21-compatible interface
X.21	Interface for synchronous operation
X.25	Interface between data terminal equipment and data circuit-terminating equipment for terminals operating in the packet-switch mode on public data networks
X.28	DTE/DCE interface for start/stop mode terminal equipment accessing a PAD on a public data network
X.29	Procedures for exchange of control information and user data between a packet mode DTE and a PAD
X.95	Network parameters in public data networks
X.96	Call progress signals in public data networks
X.121	International addressing scheme for PDNs

Appendix IV
Computer Alphabets

Four alphabets are in common use for computer communications: ASCII, also known as International Telegraphic Alphabet No. 5; Baudot, used in telex and also known as International Telegraphic Alphabet No. 2; UK Standard videotex, a variant of ASCII; and EDCDIC, used by IBM.

ASCII
This is the standard, fully implemented character set. There are a number of national variants: # in the US variant is £ in the UK variant. Many micro keyboards cannot generate all the characters directly, particularly the non-printing characters used for control of transmission, effectors of format and information separators. The 'keyboard' column gives the usual method of providing them, but you should check the firmware/software manuals for your particular set-up. You should also know that many of the 'spare' control characters are often used to enable special features on printers. The IBM PC and its clones use ASCII, not EBCDIC; they display 'non-printing' characters as graphics so you can view the full 256-character set.

HEX	DEC	ASCII	Name	Keyboard	Notes
00	0	NUL	Null	⟨ctrl⟩@	
01	1	SOH	Start heading	⟨ctrl⟩A	
02	2	STX	Start text	⟨ctrl⟩B	
03	3	ETX	End text	⟨ctrl⟩C	
04	4	EOT	End transmission	⟨ctrl⟩D	
05	5	ENQ	Enquire	⟨ctrl⟩E	
06	6	ACK	Acknowledge	⟨ctrl⟩F	
07	7	BEL	Bell	⟨ctrl⟩G	
08	8	BS	Backspace	⟨ctrl⟩H	or special key
09	9	HT	Horizontal tab	⟨ctrl⟩I	or special key
0A	10	LF	Line feed	⟨ctrl⟩J	
0B	11	VT	Vertical tab	⟨ctrl⟩K	
0C	12	FF	Form feed	⟨ctrl⟩L	
0D	13	CR	Carriage return	⟨ctrl⟩M	or special key
0E	14	SO	Shift out	⟨ctrl⟩N	

Hex	Dec	Char	Description	Key	Note
0F	15	SI	Shift in	⟨ctrl⟩O	
10	16	DLE	Data link escape	⟨ctrl⟩P	
11	17	DC1	Device control 1	⟨ctrl⟩Q	also XON
12	18	DC2	Device control 2	⟨ctrl⟩R	
13	19	DC3	Device control 3	⟨ctrl⟩S	also XOF
14	20	DC4	Device control 4	⟨ctrl⟩T	
15	21	NAK	Negative acknowledge	⟨ctrl⟩U	
16	22	SYN	Synchronous idle	⟨ctrl⟩V	
17	23	ETB	End trans, block	⟨ctrl⟩W	
18	24	CAN	Cancel	⟨ctrl⟩X	
19	25	EM	End medium	⟨ctrl⟩Y	
1A	26	SS	Special sequence	⟨ctrl⟩Z	spare
1B	27	ESC	Escape		check manuals to transmit
1C	28	FS	File separator		
1D	29	GS	Group separator		
1E	30	RS	Record seperator		
1F	31	US	Unit separator		
20	32	SP	Space		
21	33	!			
22	34	"			
23	35	#			£
24	36	$			
25	37	%			
26	38	&			
27	39	'	Apostrophe		
28	40	(			
29	41	)			
2A	42	*			
2B	43	+			
2C	44	,	Comma		
2D	45	-			
2E	46	.	Period		
2F	47	/	Slash		
30	48	0			
31	49	1			
32	50	2			
33	51	3			
34	52	4			
35	53	5			
36	54	6			
37	55	7			
38	56	8			
39	57	9			
3A	58	:	Colon		
3B	59	;	Semicolon		
3C	60	⟨			
3D	61	=			
3E	62	⟩			

3F	63	?	
40	64	@	
41	65	A	
42	66	B	
43	67	C	
44	68	D	
45	69	E	
46	70	F	
47	71	G	
48	72	H	
49	73	I	
4A	74	J	
4B	75	K	
4C	76	L	
4D	77	M	
4E	78	N	
4F	79	O	
50	80	P	
51	81	Q	
52	82	R	
53	83	S	
54	84	T	
55	85	U	
56	86	V	
57	87	W	
58	88	X	
59	89	Y	
5A	90	Z	
5B	91	[	
5C	92	\	Backslash
5D	93	]	
5E	94	^	Circumflex
5F	95	_	Underscore
60	96	`	Grave accent
61	97	a	
62	98	b	
63	99	c	
64	100	d	
65	101	e	
66	102	f	
67	103	g	
68	104	h	
69	105	i	
6A	106	j	
6B	107	k	
6C	108	l	
6D	109	m	
6E	110	n	

6F	111	o	
70	112	p	
71	113	q	
72	114	r	
73	115	s	
74	116	t	
75	117	u	
76	118	v	
77	119	w	
78	120	x	
79	121	y	
7A	122	z	
7B	123	{	
7C	124	|	
7D	125	}	
7E	126	~	Tilde
7F	127	DEL	Delete

Baudot

This is the telex/telegraphy code known to the CCITT as International Alphabet No 2. It is essentially a 5-bit code, bracketed by a start bit (space) and a stop bit (mark). Idling is shown by 'mark'. The code only supports capital letters, figures and two 'supervisory' codes: 'Bell' to warn the operator at the far end and 'WRU' – 'Who are you?' to interrogate the far end. 'Figures' changes all characters received after to their alternates, and 'Letters' switches back.

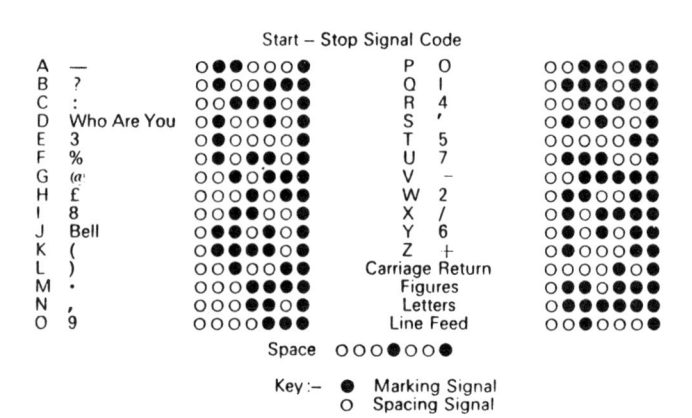

Start – Stop Signal Code

A	–	○●●○○○●	P	0	○○●●○●●
B	?	○●○○●●●	Q	1	○●●●○●●
C	:	○○●●●○●	R	4	○○●○●○●
D	Who Are You	○●○○●○●	S	'	○●○●○○●
E	3	○●○○○○●	T	5	○○○○●●●
F	%	○●○●●○●	U	7	○●●●○○●
G	@	○○●○●●●	V	–	○○●●●●●
H	£	○○○●○●●	W	2	○●●○○●●
I	8	○○●●○○●	X	/	○●○●●●●
J	Bell	○●●○●○●	Y	6	○●○○●●●
K	(	○●●●●○●	Z	+	○●○○○●●
L	)	○○●○○●●	Carriage Return		○○○○●○●
M	.	○○○●●●●	Figures		○●●○●●●
N	,	○○○●●○●	Letters		○●●●●●●
O	9	○○○○●●●	Line Feed		○○●○○○●

Space ○○○●○○●

Key :– ● Marking Signal
○ Spacing Signal

150

Videotex

This is the character set used by the UK system, which is the most widely used worldwide. The character set has many features in common with ASCII but also departs from it in significant ways, notably to provide various forms of graphics, colour controls, screen clear (‹ctrl›L), etc. The set is shared with teletext which in itself requires further special codes, for example, to enable subtitling to broadcast television, newsflash etc. If you are using proper viewdata software, then everything will display properly; if you are using a conventional terminal emulator, then the result may look confusing.

Each character consists of 10 bits:

Start	binary 0
7 bits of character code	
Parity bit	even
Stop	binary 1

ENQ (‹ctrl›E) is sent by the host on log-on to iniate the auto-log-on from the user's terminal. If no response is obtained, the user is requested to input the password manually.

Each new page sequence opens with a 'clear screen' instruction (‹ctrl›L, CHR$12) followed by a 'home' (‹ctrl›M, CHR$14).

Some viewdata services are also available via standard asynchronous 300/300 ports (Prestel is, for example); in these cases the graphics characters are stripped out and replaced by ****s; and the pages will scroll up the screen rather than present themselves in the frame-by-frame format.

The standard transmission code is shown in the table overleaf.

If you wish to edit to a viewdata system using a normal keyboard, or view a viewdata stream as it comes from a host using 'control-show' facilities, the table below gives the usual equivalents. The normal default at the left-hand side of each line is alphanumerics white. Each subsequent 'attribute', i.e. if you wish to change to colour or a variety of graphics, occupies a character space. Routing commands and signals to start and end edit depend on the software installed on the viewdata host computer: in Prestel-compatible systems, the edit page is *910#, options must be entered in lower-case letters and end edit is called by ‹esc›K.

‹esc›A	alpha red
‹esc›B	alpha green
‹esc›C	alpha yellow
‹esc›D	alpha blue

PRESTEL TRANSMISSION CODES

b8 b7 b6 b5 / b4 b3 b2 b1	0 0 0 0	0 0 0 1	0 0 1 0	0 0 1 1	0 1 0 0	0 1 0 1	0 1 1 0	0 1 1 1
COL / ROW	0	1	2	2a	3	3b	4	4b
0000 / 0	NUL		SP		0		@	
0001 / 1		CURSOR ON	!		1		A	ALPHANUMERIC RED
0010 / 2			"		2	SET VERIFY MODE (1)	B	ALPHANUMERIC GREEN
0011 / 3			£		3	SET VERIFY MODE (2)	C	ALPHANUMERIC YELLOW
0100 / 4		CURSOR OFF	$		4	SKIP BLOCK	D	ALPHANUMERIC BLUE
0101 / 5	LNQ		%		5	SET PROGRAMME MODE	E	ALPHANUMERIC MAGENTA
0110 / 6			&		6		F	ALPHANUMERIC CYAN
0111 / 7			'		7		G	ALPHANUMERIC WHITE
1000 / 8	ACTIVE POSITION BACKWARD (APB)		(		8		H	FLASH
1001 / 9	ACTIVE POSITION FORWARD (APF)		)		9		I	STEADY
1010 / 10	ACTIVE POSITION DOWN (APD)		*		:		J	
1011 / 11	ACTIVE POSITION UP (APU)	ESC	+		;		K	
1100 / 12	CLEAR SCREEN (CS)		,		<		L	NORMAL HEIGHT
1101 / 13	ACTIVE POSITION RETURN (APR)		-		=		M	DOUBLE HEIGHT
1110 / 14			.		>		N	
1111 / 15	ACTIVE POSITION HOME (APH)		/		?		O	

5	5b	6	6a	7	7a
P				p	
Q	MOSAIC RED	a		q	
R	MOSAIC GREEN	b		r	
S	MOSAIC YELLOW	c		s	
T	MOSAIC BLUE	d		t	
U	MOSAIC MAGENTA	e		u	
V	MOSAIC CYAN	f		v	
W	MOSAIC WHITE	g		w	
X	CONCEAL DISPLAY	h		x	
Y	CONTIGUOUS MOSAICS	i		y	
Z	SEPARATED MOSAICS	j		z	
[		k		→	
\	BLACK BACKGROUND	l		←	
]	NEW BACKGROUND	m		↑	
^	HOLD MOSAICS	n		-	
#	RELEASE MOSAICS	o		■	

NOTE:

COLUMNS 0 AND 1 FORM THE C0 CONTROL CHARACTER SET

COLUMNS 4b AND 5B FORM THE C1 SET OF DISPLAY ATTRIBUTE CONTROL CODES

COLUMNS 2, 3, 4, 5, 6, AND 7 FORM THE G0 CHARACTER SET

COLUMNS 2A, 3A, 4, 5, 6A AND 7A FORM THE MOSAIC CHARACTER SET. THE SHADED AREA REPRESENTS FOREGROUND COLOUR.

⟨esc⟩E	alpha magenta
⟨esc⟩F	alpha cyan
⟨esc⟩G	alpha white
⟨esc⟩H	flash
⟨esc⟩L	normal height
⟨esc⟩Y	contiguous graphics
⟨esc⟩⟨ctrl⟩D	black background
⟨esc⟩Q	graphics red
⟨esc⟩R	graphics green
⟨esc⟩S	graphics yellow
⟨esc⟩T	graphics blue
⟨esc⟩U	graphics magenta
⟨esc⟩V	graphics cyan
⟨esc⟩W	graphics white
⟨esc⟩I	steady
⟨esc⟩M	double height
⟨esc⟩Z	separated graphics
⟨esc-shift⟩M	new background (varies)
⟨esc⟩J	start edit
⟨esc⟩K	end edit

EBCDIC

The Extended Binary Coded Decimal Interchange Code is a 265-state 8-bit extended binary-coded digit code employed by IBM – except for the PC family – for internal purposes and is the only important exception to ASCII. Not all 256 codes are utilized, some being reserved for future expansion, and a number are specially identified for application-specific purposes. In transmission, it is usual to add a further digit for parity checking. Normally the transmission mode is synchronous, so there are no 'start' and 'stop' bits.

The table shows how EBCDIC compares with ASCII of the same bit configuration.

IBM control characters:

EBCDIC	bits		Notes
NUL	0000	0000	Null
SOH	0000	0001	Start of heading
STX	0000	0010	Start of text
ETX	0000	0011	End of text
PF	0000	0100	Punch off
HT	0000	0101	Horizontal tab
LC	0000	0110	Lower case

DEL	0000	0111	Delete
	0000	1000	
RLF	0000	1001	Reverse line feed
SMM	0000	1010	Start of manual message
VT	0000	1011	Vertical Tab
FF	0000	1100	Form feed
CR	0000	1101	Carriage return
SO	0000	1110	Shift out
SI	0000	1111	Shift in
DLE	0001	0000	Data link exchange
DC1	0001	0001	Device control 1
DC2	0001	0010	Device control 2
TM	0001	0011	Tape mark
RES	0001	0100	Restore
NL	0001	0101	New line
BS	0001	0110	Backspace
IL	0001	0111	Idle
CAN	0001	1000	Cancel
EM	0001	1001	End of medium
CC	0001	1010	Cursor control
CU1	0001	1011	Customer use 1
IFS	0001	1100	Interchange file separator
IGS	0001	1101	Interchange group separator
IRS	0001	1110	Interchange record separator
IUS	0001	1111	Interchange unit separator
DS	0010	0000	Digit select
SOS	0010	0001	Start of significance
FS	0010	0010	Field separator
	0010	0011	
BYP	0010	0100	Bypass
LF	0010	0101	Line feed
ETB	0010	0110	End of transmission block
ESC	0010	0111	Escape
	0010	1000	
	0010	1001	
SM	0010	1010	Set mode
CU2	0010	1011	Customer use 2
	0010	1100	
ENQ	0010	1101	Enquiry
ACK	0010	1110	Acknowledge
BEL	0010	1111	Bell
	0011	0000	
	0011	0001	
SYN	0011	0010	Synchronous idle
	0011	0011	
PN	0011	0100	Punch on
RS	0011	0101	Reader stop
UC	0011	0110	Upper case

EOT	0011 0111	End of transmission
	0011 1000	
	0011 1001	
	0011 1010	
CU3	0011 1011	Customer use 3
DC4	0011 1100	Device control 4
NAK	0011 1101	Negative acknowledge
	0011 1110	
SUB	0011 1111	Substitute
SP	0100 0000	Space
	0100 0001	

The table continues with all the printed letters and symbols. The lower-case alphabet begins at 1000 0001. The upper-case alphabet begins at 1100 0001. But there are substantial gaps for future undefined uses.

Appendix V
Modems and Services

The following table gives the standards and tones in common use. The V standards are those used in most of the world; Bell is confined largely to North America. V.22 and Bell 212A are more or less the same.

Service designator	Speed	Duplex	Transmit 0 1	Receive 0 1	Answer
V.21 orig	300*	full	1180 980	1850 1650	–
V.21 ans	300*	full	1850 1650	1180 980	2100
V.23 (1)	600	half	1700 1300	1700 1300	2100
V.23 (2)	1200	f/h†	2100 1300	2100 1300	2100
V.23 back	75	f/h†	450 390	450 390	–
Bell 103 orig	300*	full	1070 1270	2025 2225	–
Bell 103 ans	300*	full	2025 2225	1070 1270	2225
Bell 202	1200	half	2200 1200	2200 1200	2025
V.22/212A	1200	full	(see below)		
V.22 bis	2400	full	(see below)		

* Any speed up to 300 bits/s can also include 75 and 110 bits/s services.

† Service can either be half duplex at 1200 bits/s or asymmetrical full duplex, with 75 bits/s originate and 1200 bits/s receive (commonly used as viewdata user) or 1200 transmit and 75 receive (viewdata host).

Transmission at higher speeds uses different signalling techniques from the simple on-and-off keying of pairs of tones used for low-speed working. Simple tone-detection circuits cannot switch on and off sufficiently rapidly to be reliable so another method of detecting individual 'bits' has to be employed. The way it is done is by using *phase detection*. The rate of signalling doesn't go up – it stays at 600 baud – but each signal is modulated at origin by phase and then demodulated in the same way at the far end. Two channels are used, high and low, so that you can achieve bi-directional or duplex communication.

The tones are:

originate (low channel) 1200 Hz
answer (high channel) 2400 Hz

and they are the same for the European CCITT V.22 standard and for the Bell equivalent, Bell 212A. V.22 bis is the variant for 2400 bits/s full duplex transmission; there is no equivalent Bell term.

The speed differences are obtained in this way:

600 bits/s (V.22) Each bit encoded as a phase change from the previous phase. There are two possible symbols which consist of one of two phase angles; each symbol conveys 1 bit of information.

1200 bits/s (V.22 and Bell 212A) Differential phase-shift keying is used to give 4 possible symbols which consist of one of 4 phase angles. Each symbol coveys 2 bits of information to enable a 600-baud signal rate to handle 1200 bits.

2400 bits/s (V.22 bis) Quadrature amplitude modulation is used to give 16 possible symbols which consist of 12 phase angles and 3 levels of amplitude. Each symbol conveys 4 bits of information to enable a 600-baud signal rate to handle 2400 bits.

British Telecom markets the UK services under the name of Datel as follows (for simplicity the list covers only those services which use the PTSN or are otherwise easily accessible, four-wire services, for example, are excluded):

Datel	Speed	Mode	Remarks
100(H)	50	async	Teleprinters, Baudot code
100(J)	75-100	async	News services, etc., Baudot code
	50	async	Telex service, Baudot code
200	300	async	Full duplex, ASCII
400	600	async	Out-station to in-station only
600	1200		Several versions exist: for 1200 half duplex; 75/1200 for viewdata users; 1200/75 for viewdata hosts; and a rare 600 variant. The 75 speed is technically only for supervision but gives asymmetrical duplex

BT has supplied the following modems for the various services (the older ones are now available on the 'second-user' market):

Modem No. Remarks

1	1200 half duplex, massive
2	300 full duplex, massive
11	4800 synchronous, older type
12	2400/1200 synchronous
13	300 full duplex, plinth type
20(1)	1200 half duplex, 'shoe box' style
(2)	1200/75 asymetrical duplex, 'shoe box' style
(3)	75/1200 asymetrical duplex, 'shoe box' style
21	300 full duplex, modern type
22	1200 half duplex, modern type
24	4800 synchronous, modern type (made by Racal)
27A	1200 full duplex, sync or async (US-made and slightly modified from Bell 212A to CCITT tones)
27B	1200 full duplex, sync or async (UK-made)

You should note that some commercial 1200/1200 full-duplex modems also contain firmware providing ARQ error-correction protocols; modems on both ends of the line must have the facilities, of course.

BT Line Connectors

Modems can be connected directly to the BT network ('hard-wired') simply by identifying the pair that comes into the building. Normally the pair you want are the two outer wires in a standard 4 x 2 BT junction box. (The other wires are the 'return' or to support a 'ringing' circuit).

A variety of plugs and sockets have been used by BT. Until recently the standard connector for a modem was a four-ring jack, type 505, to go into a socket 95A. Prestel equipment was terminated into a similar jack, this time with five rings, which went into a socket type 96A. However, now all phones, modems, viewdata sets, etc., are terminated in the identical modular jack, type 600. The corresponding sockets need special tools to insert the line cable into the appropriate receptacles. Whatever other interconnections you see behind a socket, the two wires of the twisted pair are the ones found in the centres of the two banks of receptacles.

North America also now uses a modular jack and socket system, but not one which is physically compatible with UK designs ... did you expect otherwise?

JACK STYLE **NEW STYLE**

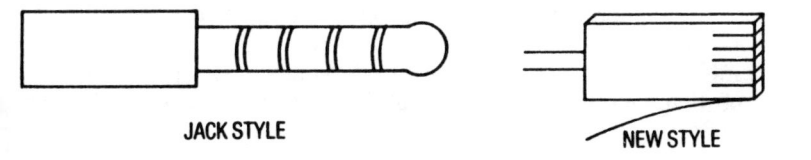

Hayes Protocols

The US firm of D.C. Hayes & Co. pioneered the idea of 'smart' or intelligent modems which could be completely commanded from a computer keyboard or from within a program. The modems include an auto-dialler, auto-answer facilities and the ability to read the status of a telephone line and report back results. Hayes is not the only company to produce such models, but, because of their early dominance of the US market, first with the Apple II and then with the IBM PC, much comms software has been written with its command set in mind. As a result other manufacturers have had to come into line.

Not all 'Hayes-compatible' modems feature all the Hayes commands; some are considered illegal in the UK, for example, because it is thought their use might tie up telephone lines for too long – repeated retrying of an engaged number is frowned on, for example. It does not seem to occur to BT officials that, even if a firmware feature is disabled, it can easily be rectified in software.

The following are the principal Hayes commands. They all begin with the charcters 'AT' and end with ‹cr›.

AT	A	Answer phone
AT	D*n*	Dial phone number *n*
AT	E0	Echo suppress characters
AT	E1	Echo show characters
AT	H0	Hang up
AT	H1	Go on line
AT	O	Force on line
AT	Q	Enable/disable result codes
AT	$	Set registers
AT	?	Read value of registers
AT	=	Set register value
AT	W0	Non-verbose result code format
AT	W1	Verbose result code format
AT	Z	Software reset

The registers set such items as the number of rings before auto-answer is enabled or the length of time that a modem will wait to hear a remote carrier tone before disconnecting itself. The result codes are messages from the modem to the computer reporting such events as 'ringing', 'connected', 'disconnected', 'no carrier', etc.

Appendix VI RS232C and V.24

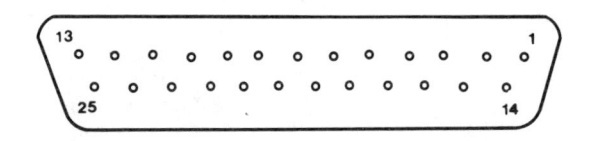

The RS232C or, to give its proper name outside the United States, CCITT Recommendation V.24, standard specifies a list of definitions for interchange circuits between data terminal equipment and data circuit-terminating equipment. More familiarly, it is the standard way of connecting a computer with a peripheral like a modem or printer where the data is passed serially, one bit at a time time, rather than in parallel format, where several bits are passed simultaneously. The RS232 cable must be the only interconnecting cable ever to have a song written about it – the 'Spitting Image' adult puppet show featured a skit on heavy metal rock with words that were a hymn of praise to RS232C. Clearly the writers were unaware of the many annoying variants to the standard which make life so difficult for computer buffs.

The only links essential to communication are transmit, receive, and signal ground. However, many micros and modems and popular comms software require other links to exist as well. The links are used to enable the computer to control the flow of data into and out from its buffer and to provide signals to the software which can trigger on-screen messages to the user like 'CONNECT' or 'CARRIER LOST'.

In its full implementation there are twenty-five lines and each may be referred to in no less than four ways, by pin number, by short-form name, by EIA (United States) code and by CCITT code (everywhere else). The table below is designed to help you identify a link by any of these systems:

Pin No.	Name	Direction*	EIA	CCITT	Notes
1	FG		AA	101	Frame protective ground
2	TD	))	BA	103	Transmitted data
3	RD	((	BB	104	Received data
4	RTS	))	CA	105	Request to send
5	CTS	((	CB	106	Clear to send
6	DSR	((	CC	107	Data set ready
7	SG		AB	102	Signal ground
8	DCD	((	CF	109	Data carrier detect
9		((			Testing + voltage
10		((			Testing − voltage
11		((	SA		Supervisory transmitted data − used in equalizing
12	SDCD	((	SCF	122	Secondary received line Signal detect − used for high-speed detect in multispeed modems
13	SCTS	((	SCB	121	
14	STD	))	SBA	118	Secondary clear to send
15	TC	((	DB	114	Secondary transmitted data Transmitter clock (synchronous protocols)
16	SRD	((	SBB	119	
17	RC	((	DD	115	Secondary received data Receiver clock (synchronous protocols)
18					
19	SSRTS	))	SCA	120	Unassigned
20	DTR	))	CD	108.2	Secondary request to send
21	SQ	((	CG	110	Data terminal ready
22	RI	((	CE	125	Signal quality detector Ring indicator (for auto-answer)
23		))	CH	111	Data rate selector
		((	CI	112	Ditto
24	ETC	))	DA	113	External transmitter clock (synchronous protocols)
25		))			Unassigned

* The 'Direction' column shows the direction of data flow

BT modems tend to use the CCITT nomenclature on their status lights; other manufacturers use almost anything: Tx and Rx are transmit and receive respectively; CD often means 'carrier detect' (i.e. line seized and appropriate remote modem tone being heard).

Many personal micros do not use the full RS 232C

implemenation and, in particular, adopt different physical connectors. (Even the IBM AT now uses a 9-pin D connector instead of the 25-pin).

Appendix VII
The Radio Spectrum

The following table gives the allocation of the radio frequency spectrum up to 30 MHz. The bands in which radio-teletype and radio-data traffic are most common are those allocated to 'fixed' services, but data traffic is also found in the amateur and maritime bands. In the official publication (see below) 'government' services include military traffic as well as those belonging to civilian government agencies. Aeronautical (R) means aircraft travelling along recognized civil aircraft routes; aeronautical (OR) means off-route aircraft – these are nearly always military. Do not expect to make much sense of non-civilian radio traffic!

VLF, MF, HF, Radio Frequency Spectrum Table

9	–	14	Radio navigation
14	–	19.95	Fixed/maritime mobile
20			Standard frequency and time
20.05	–	70	Fixed and maritime mobile
70	–	90	Fixed/maritime mobile/radio navigation
90	–	110	Radio navigation
110	–	130	Fixed/maritime mobile/radio navigation
130	–	148.5	Maritime mobile/fixed
148.5	–	255	Broadcasting
255	–	283.5	Broadcasting/radio navigation (aero)
283.5	–	315	Maritime/aeronautical navigation
315	–	325	Aeronautical radio navigation/maritime radio beacons
325	–	405	Aeronautical radio navigation
405	–	415	Radio navigation (410 = DF)
415	–	495	Aeronautical radio navigation/maritime mobile
495	–	505	Mobile (distress and calling) – ›500: CW and RTTY
505	–	526.5	Maritime mobile/aeronautical navigation
526.5	–	1606.5	Broadcasting
1606.5	–	1625	Maritime mobile/fixed/land mobile
1625	–	1635	Radio location

1635 – 1800	Maritime mobile/fixed/land mobile
1800 – 1810	Radio location
1810 – 1850	Amateur
1850 – 2000	Fixed/mobile
2000 – 2045	Fixed/mobile
2045 – 2160	Maritime mobile/fixed/land mobile
2160 – 2170	Radio location
2170 – 2173.5	Maritime mobile
2173.5 – 2190.5	Mobile (distress and calling) – ›2182: voice
2190.5 – 2194	Maritime and mobile
2194 – 2300	Fixed and mobile
2300 – 2498	Fixed/mobile/broadcasting
2498 – 2502	Standard frequency and time
2502 – 2650	Maritime mobile/maritime radio navigation
2650 – 2850	Fixed/mobile
2850 – 3025	Aeronautical mobile (R)
3025 – 3155	Aeronautical mobile (OR)
3155 – 3200	Fixed/mobile/low power hearing aids
3200 – 3230	Fixed/mobile/broadcasting
3230 – 3400	Fixed/mobile/broadcasting
3400 – 3500	Aeronautical mobile (R)
3500 – 3800	Amateur/fixed/mobile
3800 – 3900	Fixed/aeronautical mobile (OR)
3900 – 3930	Aeronautical mobile (OR)
3930 – 4000	Fixed/broadcasting
4000 – 4063	Fixed/maritime mobile
4063 – 4438	Maritime mobile
4438 – 4650	Fixed/mobile
4650 – 4700	Aeronautical mobile (R)
4700 – 4750	Aeronautical mobile (OR)
4750 – 4850	Fixed/aeronautical mobile (OR)/land mobile/broadcasting
4850 – 4995	Fixed/land mobile/broadcasting
4995 – 5005	Standard frequency and time
5005 – 5060	Fixed/broadcasting
5060 – 5450	Fixed/mobile
5450 – 5480	Fixed/aeronautical mobile (OR)/land mobile
5480 – 5680	Aeronautical mobile (R)
5680 – 5730	Aeronautical mobile (OR)
5730 – 5950	Fixed/land mobile
5950 – 6200	Broadcasting
6200 – 6525	Maritime mobile
6525 – 6685	Aeronautical mobile (R)
6685 – 6765	Aeronautical mobile (OR)
6765 – 6795	Fixed/ISM

7000	–	7100	Amateur
7100	–	7300	Broadcasting
7300	–	8100	Maritime mobile
8100	–	8195	Fixed/maritime mobile
8195	–	8815	Maritime mobile
8815	–	8965	Aeronautical mobile (R)
8965	–	9040	Aeronautical mobile (OR)
9040	–	9500	Fixed
9500	–	9900	Broadcasting
9900	–	9995	Fixed
9995	–	10005	Standard frequency and time
10005	–	10100	Aeronautical mobile (R)
10100	–	10150	Fixed/amateur (sec.)
10150	–	11175	Fixed
11175	–	11275	Aeronautical mobile (OR)
11275	–	11400	Aeronautical mobile (R)
11400	–	11650	Fixed
11650	–	12050	Broadcasting
12050	–	12230	Fixed
12230	–	13200	Maritime mobile
13200	–	13260	Aeronautical mobile (OR)
13260	–	13360	Aeronautical mobile (R)
13360	–	13410	Fixed/radio astronomy
13410	–	13600	Fixed
13600	–	13800	Broadcasting
13800	–	14000	Fixed
14000	–	14350	Amateur
14350	–	14990	Fixed
14990	–	15010	Standard frequency and time
15010	–	15100	Aeronautical mobile (OR)
15100	–	15600	Broadcasting
15600	–	16360	Fixed
16360	–	17410	Maritime mobile
17410	–	17550	Fixed
17550	–	17900	Broadcasting
17900	–	17970	Aeronautical mobile (R)
17970	–	18030	Aeronautical mobile (OR)
18030	–	18052	Fixed
18052	–	18068	Fixed/space research
18068	–	18168	Amateur
18168	–	18780	Fixed
18780	–	18900	Maritime mobile
18900	–	19680	Fixed
19680	–	19800	Maritime mobile
19800	–	19990	Fixed
19990	–	20010	Standard frequency and time
20010	–	21000	Fixed
21000	–	21450	Amateur

21450	–	21850	Broadcasting
21850	–	21870	Fixed
21870	–	21924	Aeronautical fixed
21924	–	22000	Aeronautical (R)
22000	–	22855	Maritime mobile
22855	–	23200	Fixed
23200	–	23350	Aeronautical fixed and mobile (R)
23350	–	24000	Fixed/mobile
24000	–	24890	Fixed/land mobile
24890	–	24990	Amateur
24990	–	25010	Standard frequency and time
25010	–	25070	Fixed/mobile
25070	–	25210	Maritime mobile
25210	–	25550	Fixed/mobile
25550	–	25670	Radio astronomy
25670	–	26100	Broadcasting
26100	–	26175	Maritime mobile
26175	–	27500	Fixed/mobile (CB) (26.975-27.2835 ISM)
27500	–	28000	Meteorological aids/fixed/mobile (CB)
28000	–	29700	Amateur
29700	–	30005	Fixed/mobile

These allocations are as they apply in Europe; slight variations occur in other regions of the globe. More information can be obtained from *The United Kingdom Table of Frequency Allocations*, HMSO for the Department of Trade and Industry Radio Regulatory Division.

Frequencies for specific services may be found in *Guide to RTTY Frequencies* and *Confidential Frequency List* both published by Gilfer Associates Inc., PO Box 239, 52 Park Avenue, Ridge, NJ 07656, USA, and *Klingenfuss Utility Guide*, available from Panoramastrasse 81, D-7400 Tübingen, Federal Republic of Germany.

Appendix VIII
Port-Finder Flow chart

This flow chart will enable owners of auto-diallers to carry out an automatic search of a range of telephone numbers to determine which of them have modems hanging off the back.

It is a flow chart and not a program listing, because the whole exercise is very hardware-dependent: you will have to determine what sort of instructions and in what form your auto-modem will accept; you must also see what sort of signals it can send back to your computer so that your program can 'read' them.

You will also need to devise some ways of sensing the phone line, whether it has been seized, whether you are getting 'ringing', if there is an engaged tone, a voice, a number-obtainable tone or a modem whistle. Most 'smart' modems have these functions built in, but the command set required to make a program work varies from machine to machine (see appendix V).

Line-seizure detect, if not already available on your modem, is simply a question of reading the phone line voltage; the other conditions can be detected with simple tone decoder modules based on the 567 chip. The lines from these detectors should then be brought to a A/D board which your computer software can scan and read.

PORT-FINDER FLOW CHART

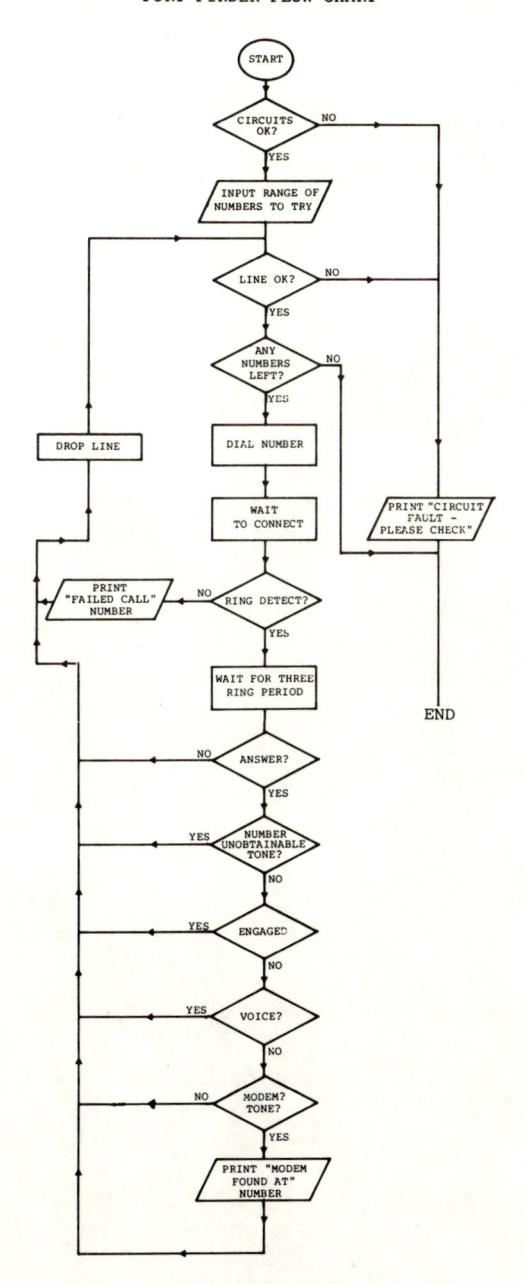